Reconnecting With Celtic Trees

by Jackie Queally

RECONNECTING WITH CELTIC TREES
First Edition 2017

Copyright 2017 by Jackie Queally

Graphics by Tanya Harris
Cover images and interior images by Nicola Moss
Book design by Ivan Andfelovski
Front cover image: The Augurs Oak by Nicola Moss 1995 oil painting 45cm×61cm
Back cover image: Drum Tree by Nicola Moss 1996 bronze plaque 21cm×16cm

All rights reserved. This book or any portion thereof may not be reproduced or used in any manner whatsoever without the express written permission of the publisher except for the use of brief quotations in a book review.

Printed by Lightning Source in the United Kingdom

Published by Earthwise Publications

ISBN 978-0-9930512-5-8

Earthwise Publications,
Gort,
Co Galway,
Ireland

www.earthwise.me

Other Titles by Jackie Queally

Tree Murmurs
Rosslyn Chapel and Hinterland
The Lothians Unveiled
The Culdees
The Spiritual Meaning of Rosslyn's Carvings
The Spiritual Purpose to Rosslyn
Arks within Grail Lands
Eternal Elements
Spirit of the Burren
Essence of the Burren
The Burren Trails

All available on Amazon and easily ordered in shops,
or can be bought directly from author at *www.earthwise.me/shop/*

Please request a signed copy by emailing *jackiequeally@gmail.com*

"Meditations, affirmations, rituals and insights galore here to help us re-connect with trees. In Gaelic Ireland, the sacred tree was known as a 'bile'. You would have found it inside a fort or near a holy well. It might have been an oak, that mighty tree which is associated with countless place names in Ireland. Such was the symbolic force of the word 'bile' that it could be used, figuratively, to describe someone of blemishless, upright character: *a bhile gan chealg*, you are a true oak!

When Ireland became denuded of her forests and woodlands - to build stout ships for the British Navy and other noble purposes - such plunder was an economic, environmental and spiritual loss to the country and in such songs as *Cill Chais*, poets bewailed this incalculable loss: *cad a dhé-an-faimid feasta gan adhmad*, 'what shall we do without timber'? This book can assist us with the necessary process of collective healing and help others around the world who are witnessing the calamitous loss of trees."

Gabriel Rosenstock, Irish poet and writer, Ireland

http://roghaghabriel.blogspot.ie/

http://www.amazon.co.uk/s/ref=nb_sb_noss?url=search-alias%3Dstripbooks&field-keywords=gabriel+rosenstock

Acknowledgements

Thank you very much to Diane Morrison for proof-reading my book. Her eye for detail and her meticulous approach hopefully benefit the reader! She responded to a general plea in one of my newsletters for help and I got the perfect companion for the job. Ask and ye shall receive they say. I am truly grateful. Without her constant attention at the editing stage I cannot envisage how this book would have made it to the final stage.

Thank you to Tanya Harris for her encouragement to share Gaia Touch exercises with a wider audience in County Clare.

Thank you to a dear friend, Nicola Moss for sharing some of her wonderful art for use both on the book cover and within the meditation section. Nicky's art work accompanies the poems blissfully. She is one of the most talented artists I know. Her insights now bless my book.

I would also like to acknowledge Jacqueline Memory Paterson, gifted author of *Tree Wisdom*, whose sharing of Ash mythology inspired my Ash meditation. During this meditation a red squirrel did indeed appear upon striking the ash tree with my tuning fork, and it continued to scamper around me for a long time! This to me confirms the power of myths still.

Thank you Ivan Andjelovski in Serbia who I immediately picked to do the design layout of the book. He was an absolute treat to work with and can be contacted via *www.freelancer.com*.

Thank you to Marko Pogacnik for giving permission for his exercises to be reproduced in the Gaia Touch chapter.

Thanks to friends who waited patiently to spend time with me when I was busy on the book. I thank you all for being in my life.

Table of Contents

FOREWORD 1

Chapter 1 WHY RECONNECT WITH TREES? 3

Chapter 2 THE CELTIC TREE CYCLE 7

Chapter 3 DANCE OF THE YEAR: A Series of Meditations 13

Chapter 4 FLOW OF THE YEAR 69

Chapter 5 THE ENERGETICS OF SOUND 87

Chapter 6 GAIA TOUCH WITH TREES 97

Chapter 7 FESTIVAL WALKS 107

Chapter 8 DOWSING 111

Chapter 9 THE KNOWLEDGE CONTINUUM 113

CONCLUDING REMARKS 133

APPENDIX 135

Foreword

2016 was a year of intense energies and rapid change for many in the world. I was drawn to rediscovering my moon nature. My probings took me from tree essences to new moon meditations to revisiting the Celtic Tree calendar. I had undertaken a topical study into the alleged Celtic Tree calendar twenty five years ago. I felt an intense affinity with the metaphysical belief system around these native trees. Could an old belief system perhaps practised by the Druids be a valid tool for the world we live in now? Following an inner prompt I started to explore in depth the lunar cycle of the Celtic Trees. I began with creating a meditation for each tree on a lunar monthly basis. I was not so familiar with the lunar cycle as the solar cycle presented by our modern calendar. The process taught me many things. During this time of personal creativity I was invited to Nova Scotia, Canada to lead a series of workshops on the Celtic Trees. This invitation from unlikely quarters came at exactly the right moment. I recognized "the call" and accepted. In those workshops I helped people make a more conscious connection with trees. The workshops provided a platform for me to explore my own knowing more, and it also created valuable time and space for much precious sharing of insights and experiences. Out of that wonderful work visit, I recognized there was another book to write. I wanted to write a unique book on the Celtic Trees that would offer insights into our potential as human beings.

In gathering my thoughts together for what to include in the book, I recognized more fully that the native Celtic Tree calendar offers a spiritual model for growth, rather like an Enneagram reading may suggest our way forward in life. I also could see that if we utilized our power of imagination, we could discover new parts of our inner selves through engaging with the tree archetypes. I sense that the trees, like us, are evolving.

Trees have been on the Earth far longer than we have. They have a capacity to serve as bridges between the elemental and human realms. They also connect to the "causal realm", a term coined by my friend, the geomancer and artist Marko Pogacnik. Since my student days in the 1970s I have sensed the pain that the Earth is undergoing due to human destruction of its living organisms. Many environmental groups try to ameliorate conditions, but a different path has always called me. It involves working on subtle energy levels with nature. I experienced a nagging spiritual tug to reconnect with the trees. This is a chronicle so far of my efforts to do so. Collective efforts work best, and so I hope the book will encourage groups of friends to visit their local trees.

My hope is that we learn to create a new symbiotic relationship between nature and humans. This is an essential part of the process of becoming a "new Earth". There are no experts on this journey. There are many gifted beings whose work with nature is sacred, driven by their vision and intent. I hope the following pages encourage every reader to find their own way forward, and to share it with others.

Chapter 1

WHY RECONNECT WITH TREES?

MUCH OF THE WORLD IS increasingly disconnected from nature and the living Earth, known as Gaia. Simultaneously, the world is going through a vast transition that begs a new attitude from our leaders in my view. In the new world reality that is forming, we will more fully realise that every sentient being is connected to one another. Some of us already sense this deep interconnectivity. Natural objects such as trees, animals, people, angels and the Sidhe (high fairy spirits) are interconnected in very real ways. My wise friend Marko Pogacnik, a gifted writer on how to co-create with nature, maintains we are called upon to forge a new, more living, relationship with Nature. Then we can evolve as a species in a wholesome and soulful manner.

Since I have always felt a great affinity with trees, and since there is a ready connection in general between trees and humans, I felt a need to revisit the Celtic Trees that feel part of my Irish blood heritage. They play a vital spiritual role now in upgrading the sentient life of the planet. In my small but perhaps significant experience of leading tree workshops, I have come to realise that people relate in deep and meaningful ways with trees. I also realise that trees are extremely sentient. When we relate to the trees, the trees in return do sense our loving attention and are more likely to thrive, despite the environmental duress they are under. Now more than ever is the time to give from our hearts to Gaia, the living Earth.

There is much to be said for developing a conscious connection with trees. Any natural empathy that you develop with the trees will return you benefits, such as improving your life force, or Chi, and grounding you. Everyone can improve their sense of well-being by tapping into the natural energies of trees. Moreover, trees can affect your inner growth. The manner in which this growth manifests will naturally vary from person to person. We can never demand that the trees return us their blessings. It is an act of grace. Such processes in nature make life richer and more worthwhile.

Someone once asked me what we receive in return for emotionally caring for nature. In reply I emphasized the two-way process involved between the trees and ourselves. When we acknowledge and send positive emotions to the trees, we reach out to the tree elementals too. These elementals in turn connect with other elementals who support our own well-being. It is an overlooked spiritual fact that elementals support us as much as the angels. They strengthen our life forces and assist our inner growth.

According to Marko Pogacnik, we all own elemental as well as physical bodies. His Gaia Touch exercises awaken our elemental bodies. On a soul level, our elemental bodies connect with our individual souls. I sense my tree meditations in the book can work on a soul level. I have developed a few tools to connect with the trees so as to work at this mysterious yet satisfying soul level. Meditation exercises can bring us to a soul awareness of our many dimensions. When we work consciously with our energy centres, we work with the Chi (otherwise known as Qi), the etheric energy that surrounds our physical bodies. As we become aware of our energy field, we may start to feel the movement of our souls, which reside at a deep level within our being.

Disciplines from around the world, such as Qi Gong, do much to inform us of our multi-layered dimensionality. They concentrate on embodying the awareness. I use Gaia Touch exercises to embody subtle energies that surround us, linking with other dimensions. The three lower chakras, or energy centres, in our bodies connect as follows:

- Solar Plexus — the soul unites here with our Elemental body. The soul guides our Elemental body so that it can strengthen us as a vehicle of light.
- Navel Chakra — the cosmic pulse in Gaia's womb nourishes us here.

- Base Chakra — this is where we connect with the magnetic resonance of the Earth. The resonance fluctuates. This in turn dictates the quality of the Earth's energy field. The composite layers of the Earth's energy field are known as Gaia. We synchronize our inner clocks, rhythms and presence with Gaia night and day.

Through working with Gaia Touch exercises and sound therapy, we actively strengthen our chakras and our own etheric field of energy. Our souls start to engage in a two-way process with the elementals. The activities I introduce in the book can bring inner peace and tranquility. With inner peace, success is more likely in whatever endeavour you choose to undertake.

On my "slow tours" in the west of Ireland I have been using sound healing, dowsing and Gaia Touch exercises as a means of assisting others to reconnect with nature in an efficient manner. In the following chapters I will give examples of these. Often I choose the exercises within the context of the site and client(s). Each site generates a different response in us, and so I "read" the site for its unique contribution to the general human energy field, bearing in mind we also have individual patterns.

Sound necessitates full attention in the present moment. You cannot engage in listening with a busy mind! I have used many of the sound techniques in individual healing sessions also. I found that sound therapy affects both humans and nature in a similar way. The gong and the drum have different roles. The tuning forks work with the human voice to confirm for me the tones to use with particular trees. I use forks in a similar fashion to how I dowse with rods or pendulums.

I find that dowsing (also known as divining) is a great tool for measuring the effects of our exercises. For instance, you can dowse to measure a tree's auric field to check the effects of your active communicating. I also teach people to dowse water and energy lines in the land. Dowsing complements both Sound/Vibrational work and Gaia Touch. All the activities work upon people in a similar fashion, encouraging them to be fully present. Dowsing invariably slows people down. It brings them into a different frequency where time is not rushing by. They often report losing a sense of time, and an increased sense of the more subtle dimensions that our intellects tend to ignore.

In subsequent chapters I will give some examples and an explanation of the processes involved. I feel it is important to emphasize the following. When we reconnect with trees, we are adopting an excellent grounding, or earthing, method. Since the cosmic energies are escalating it is very good practice to remain earthed. This allows us maximum chance of assimilating the higher incoming energies. Without regularly grounding ourselves, we can easily develop unhealthy patterns in our etheric fields. It is wise to maintain a healthy etheric energy field during this time of intense transition.

Chapter 2

THE CELTIC TREE CYCLE

U P TO NOW WE HAVE been considering the tree kingdom in general and how it is beneficial for both humans and nature if humans make efforts to reconnect with trees. In addition to the generic trees, there is a distinct group of trees with universal appeal that I mentioned previously; the Celtic Trees. Ireland and Britain have a long and rich tradition with their indigenous trees. They are commonly known as the Celtic Trees, and much folklore and legend testify to their significance in past Celtic cultures. I developed an interest in this when I was invited to give a talk on the subject as part of an artist's exhibition on trees during the Edinburgh Festival in 1998. For me, investigating the Celtic Trees helped me engage personally with both individual and specific groups of trees. I felt at home with the topic, and I related to the tree archetypes with a readiness beyond what current book knowledge offered. I rekindled and deepened this interest in the last year or so. Through developing my ideas and experiences into this book, I have found the discipline to address personal issues too. This is because each of the Celtic Trees is associated with certain soul qualities.

The notion of the Celtic Trees was primarily brought into international focus in recent decades with the research of Robert Graves. He wrote the illuminating book *The White Goddess* which was first published in 1948. He introduced the notion of a whole year cycle in which there were thirteen lunar months named after trees, and five seasons likewise named. He based his theory on a very rare book Ogygia written by Roderick O'Flaherty 200 years previously. Ancient Irish and Welsh poems also seem to support the idea of native trees creating a lunar calendar. These were runes etched on pieces of stone or wood. He interpreted the runes to represent the initial sounds for each tree. Here is the full range of Ogham lettering, or runes:

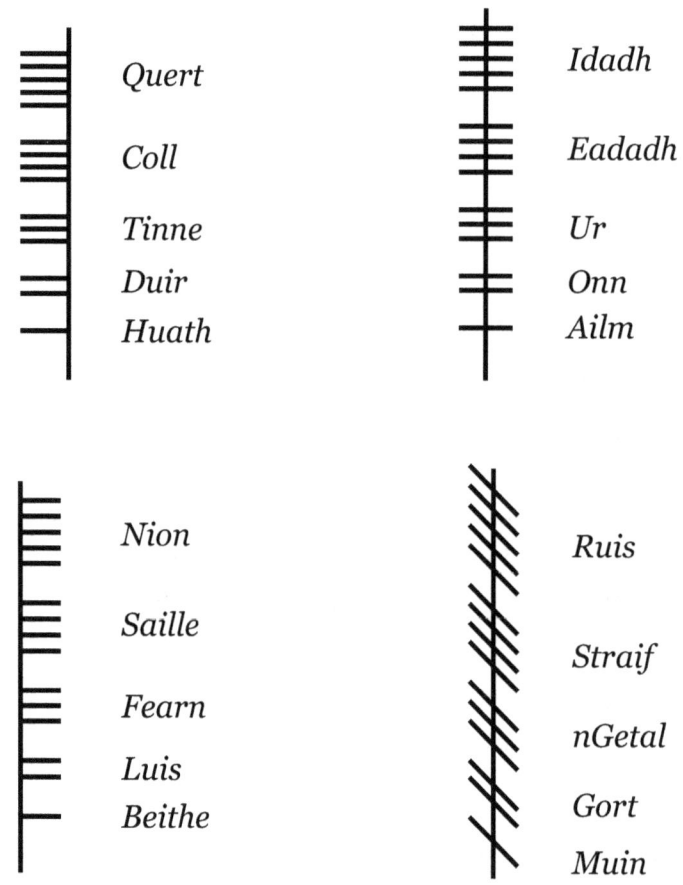

Some of the lunar months had two trees ascribed to them as the starting consonants of the Gaelic names occasionally doubled.

e.g. S = Saille (Willow) and SS = Straif (Blackthorn)

The Ogham alphabet consisted of four groups of glyphs, each bearing up to five strokes. The vowels crossed the line at right angles. (The right angle suggests a portrayal of a definite dimensional shift). The dental/aspirant letters (H D T C Q) had the strokes on the left of the line. Five of the eight noble trees were in this group: the hawthorn, oak, holly, hazel and apple. The labial letters (B L F S N) included the other main noble trees: the birch, rowan and alder. The guttural letters (M G NG ST and R) had their strokes crossing the line obliquely. There were also some other glyphs, which may have been vowel clusters.

While scholars will argue that Graves has no basis to formulate a Celtic Tree calendar it is obvious to me from a clairsentient viewpoint that he was a valid seeker and a mystic. Those who work with plant medicine have created new models that vary to some extent from his model, but Graves is responsible for the general idea of the trees relating within one whole to the unfolding of the year. Why is it important to reconnect with Celtic Trees? By understanding their rich complexities, it helps us re-establish a respect for the trees. It helps us to understand how these trees related to the wider cosmos, of which we are part. In this chapter I will introduce this holistic tree-based model that the Celts indeed may have used. I am also using the model as a springboard for inner change and awakening of consciousness. If we can imagine a cosmic viewpoint in which all trees are related to aspects of our human life, our emotional sense of belonging to a wider universe deepens. In terms of the future of our planet, this can only bode well for us. This is particularly poignant when we consider how our cosmos is actually shifting into a new paradigm. As this occurs, new insights into models such as the Celtic Tree system may help us think and create anew in our lives. In truth, I wish to "upgrade" the Celtic Tree cycle by inviting you to participate in meditations, hands-on exercises and contemplation on our shared heritage: the Celtic Trees.

In Celtic times, astronomers recognized a "Golden Year". This was precisely 18.61 years. It equated with the length of time Druids took to complete their training. It also marked the period of time required for the solar and lunar movements to briefly coincide.

The Celtic Trees fitted into a yearly cycle that involved both lunar and solar movements. The Celtic festivals celebrated solar events, while the months celebrated lunar cycles. All the dates are fluid.

The astronomical solstices and equinoxes vary from year to year, so the dates for the solstices and equinoxes adjust accordingly. The cross quarter-lies that lie midway between the solstices and equinoxes thus vary too.

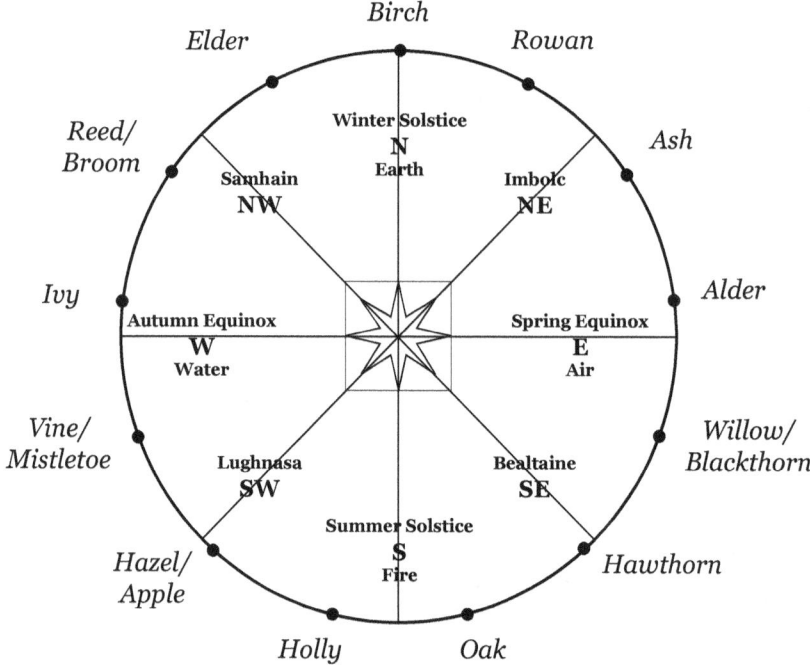

The Lunar Year with its seasonal cohorts, consonants and vowels

The cross quarterlies are Imbolc, Beltaine, Lughnassa and Samhain. They are very powerful times of year and many Neolithic monuments display astronomical alignments with these events. The above digram includes the eight festivals, the lunar months and the seasons.

In the past, a ruling class of Druids focused on deep philosophical matters. Theirs was a sophisticated and stratified society. They used their natural forest environment to provide them with an elaborate, yet secure, platform for their philosophy and world view. I get the feeling that the inner and outer worlds collided to a large degree in their teachings. The ancients' communication with the trees inspired a unique model of tree types. The model offered a psycho-spiritual template for the human soul's evolution. I discovered this when I embarked on my series of tree meditations based on the Celtic Tree year. I realized that the Celtic Tree calendar exists on an etheric level as well as on a physical one. It is not a simple matter of isolating each tree and ascribing it qualities. Each tree flows into another, responding to the previous one and preparing the way for the next. Often male and female attributes follow each other in the cycle. It is like reading a piece of classical music in which there are many counterpoints. There is a kind of dance to the calendar year, where light and darkness alternate. At opportune moments, themes reunite. I invite you to delve into a deep contemplation of the Celtic Trees. It could strengthen you, even pointing towards a progression of your soul into a new cycle.

Chapter 3

DANCE OF THE YEAR:
A Series of Meditations

THE HEART OF MY WORK lies in poetry and the imagination. The notion of the Celtic Tree year acts as a springboard for the following meditations that I created. I wish to reiterate that there is no historical hard-core evidence that the Ogham alphabet as part of a Druid calendar was consciously worked with. However, I have found that it works as a spiritual model. In other words, it works on your dreamtime, your imagination, and even your soul. It stimulates inner and outer work with trees and has the power to transform. I remember having a lucid dream of certain qualities. When I awoke, I realised that I had dreamt the feeling that the Oak contains and imparts. I was due to start conceiving the Oak meditation in the next few days, and my subconscious had fed me the Oak's inner qualities. I felt moved by this experience and felt it was a sign I was on the right track, composing these meditations on a monthly basis.

Each tree begins with a poem I wrote some years ago on its essence, followed by a guided meditation I created recently. Take note of which vowel you resonate with most. This may well reflect your underlying constitution. I have trained in TCM and realize that the vowel trees can align with each of their main five elements. One way in which you can work with the trees is to take their essences to balance yourself. (I describe the tree essences later in this book.) You may receive a free copy of my pre-recorded files for each meditation by emailing me at *info@earthwise.me* or *jackiequeally@gmail.com*. Please write COMPLEMENTARY in the header and let me know where you bought your copy of the book.

Let's start with the vowels since they seem to determine the mood of the prevailing lunar months.

Elm Season – A – Ailm (Early Spring)

I prolong
The dense quietness
That binds us to this Earth.
I follow on with destiny
The wheel that leads to rebirth
The Tree of Life.

I thrive in open spaces
Or shady streams.
A flourishing of limbs

Dance of The Year: A Series of Meditations

> Sensing space, ascending
> In glorious sweeps, descending
> In benign swoops, bowing
> To forager's delight.
>
> A simple grace
> Now rare,
> That scoops the air.
> I descendent of Eden
> Reserve
> My place.

Meditation

Breathe gently and let your body go light and flowing. Imagine your skin loosen against your body and feel the water float inside your body. Let the water wash through you, purifying you, sending love and light to all your veins and arteries. Imagine your heart sending out its own rays of light to the earth around you. Let the light pour from your heart into the earth. As long as you remain connected to the earth, you are calm and able to breathe in a nice, flowing manner. Sense how it is to become very still. As you remain still, do not become so still that you stagnate. Activate yourself. Send rays of light from your heart into your mind. Feel how the rays provide direction to your fertile mind. Know that this small movement will help you fulfill your dreams. Without a connection to love, you will not move out of the false protection of your shell.

When the heart is sending a constant flow of rays to your mind, ask yourself the question: "What is it I want to do next with my life?" If no reply comes, ask the elves for help. Listen to the reply. Observe it, and check if any fear has come in. Is this fear a reaction to the notion of taking action? If fear does arise, keep breathing, remembering your connection from your heart through your body to the earth, and from your heart to your mind. Both directions are needed. Practice visualizing that dual flow of energy for as long as you feel you need.

Affirmation

My stillness will move into action when the time is right.

Gorse Season – O – Onn (Late Spring)

I occupy the eternal souls of youth
Whose lessons are cloaked in adversity
And fruits are bruised with sweetness
For the bees

Delicate blooms of yellow brightness
Enveloped by the goddess'
Coconut-sweet breathing
Eternal in her love.

Ah! I am vigour! Ferocious fire,
Stubborn fire,
Borne of stubborn wood stems
Star-leaved in their nakedness,

Live on…

Meditation

Now Spring has begun, you stand firm and ready to grow in the warmth that approaches. This is the time when your breath and your thoughts naturally quicken. Breathe in and out, and as you do so, watch your breath, and wait until it slows down naturally. Often when we watch our breath it automatically becomes slower and steadier. This is the breath of the confident warrior who has prepared inwardly, with the help of his lunar consorts the Willow and the Blackthorn.

Focus on your breathing, watching how your thoughts follow the breath. Are they becoming less scattered, more focused, or even absent? When you feel ready, continue. Imagine you are imbibing the fiery energy of the gorse bush. Feel its power in your core, as you stand firmly on the terrain. In your mind's eye, keep varying the surroundings, so you stand in contrasting rough and smooth ground. Wherever you stand, tap into that capacity to embrace that fire within you. Your limbs can accept this fire. Open your heart to the core values you proudly possess. Let your heart soar and carry you along. Sense your passion for life rise and burn now. You are unique, and recognition of your talents comes easily, Feel pride in your own efforts, and feel ready to act boldly and decisively.

Behind your actions, there is an eternal goddess protecting you. She comes from midwinter, and is your causal self. Imagine now breathing into the back of your heart, where you meet the goddess, clothed from head to toe in beautiful green robes. Her hair hangs in long, golden tresses. She exudes a most delicate perfume, the trademark of her eternal presence. She blows you tender kisses that enter and spin inside your body, so you can bear the fruits of her loving thoughts. From her fairy blood she manifests many clusters of kiss-shaped, sunshine yellow flowers.

Bees flock to your blooms, which create a honey sweeter than clover. There can be nothing but success and profusion on your path. Feel the strength of who you are, and turn now to the journey. Set yourself a goal you previously thought was difficult, and imagine the successful outcome of that goal. Remember you are strong.

How do you feel about the obstacles you may encounter on the way to achieving your goal? Your ability to burn ferociously in the presence of all obstacles will get you through this mire.

Are there any conflicts you still fear or shy away from in your life when you imagine this battle?

Acknowledge your doubts, your own contradictions, and know they are there for a purpose. You can rise above them when you allow yourself the time and energy to go through your own turmoil. It is like a meadow. Imagine a meadow that is over-run with untidy grasses and thistles. As the mower moves through the meadow, the thistles fall and reveal an oasis of calm beauty lying beneath the mess. The meadow is your arena, your responsibility. Derive pleasure from the act of mowing down the thistles, and doing your best. It is all you can do. It is the effort you make that counts in your soul, not whether the meadow is restored permanently or not. Realise there are others beside you who will try to save the meadow. What concerns you is your own ability, your willingness to engage, using your talents. In the action lies your strength. Further, there can be no progress in these uncertain times by burrowing yourself into a hole. There can be great success if you accept where you are, what you have to offer, and move with it in the spirit of service, always loving your unique self.

Let the golden flowers and the spiky evergreens of the gorse show the way for all - as they sing of the coming seasonal light and the opportunities it brings.

Affirmation

My battles are nothing without the elementals by my side. They guide my victory.

Heather Season – U – Ura (High Summer)

Dream on
Diviner of Secrets. I am the flow for
Your optimistic surrender.
I guide your juices
Until
Love manifests
In all its myriad forms.

Meditation

You could lie down for this guided meditation. When you are comfortable, imagine you can feel the soft blooms of the heather beneath you. See if you can follow your in-breath and out-breath as your mind carries on in the background. Surrender to the fey or fairy folk who are near the surface at this time of year. Now is not the time to make plans, or to think clearly. As you watch your thoughts drift by, let them pass like clouds in a summer sky. Enjoy the space your thoughts come into. If a happy thought comes into your mind, try not to react. If an unhappy thought springs into being, let it pass too. The idea is to surrender to the dream-like consciousness we all possess. Give it space to reveal itself to us. Don't plan on doing anything with the thoughts that come in. They do not need our intervention. Know that in just accepting your thoughts as they come and go, you are practicing acceptance and balancing out your tendency to go outward at this time of year. By allowing your mind the space to just drift without a sail on the seas of your imagination, you are actually supporting a new way of being that allows the subtle mind to take over more.

Imagine now you are chasing an essence of a thought that can give rise to an action. Let it pop up on your horizon. Leave it drift to and fro across the landscape you create in your mind. As it moves, it grows in strength and power. Whenever you approach it to claim it as your own, and to steer it toward a goal, it withers. Know that the best thing is to let it be. After a while you feel a sense of well-being inside.

If you find yourself wishing to follow up a thought and make plans, particularly if it keeps cropping up, just send the thought into a black magician's hat of tricks that you see on a table in your mind's eye. By returning the thoughts rather than working on them with your ego, you are asking that the devic beings bless your work with their own action lines that are more understanding of the natural order of life. These devic beings are nursing you now in the pulse of their home. They are encouraging you to just be.

You feel you are learning to just be for a change, and you also know that what is yours will not pass you by. So let the thoughts be, and try not to follow them through to logical conclusions. In this way, you can become a new type of explorer who understands the power of the mind on outcomes in the human arena.

The thoughts that come and go now are not wasted. They come from the cosmos, guided by the fey. Spirits on the inner planes recycle these thoughts through you into right action. Surrender to their presence, for they work according to divine will. Do not be afraid to dream a while, without a need for recompense and without any reward for your efforts. Dreaming is cooling for all your warm thoughts. It is the out-breath you require.

Affirmation
I welcome the thoughts and dreams sent by the fairy world to help me grow in love.

Aspen Season – E – Eadha (Autumn)

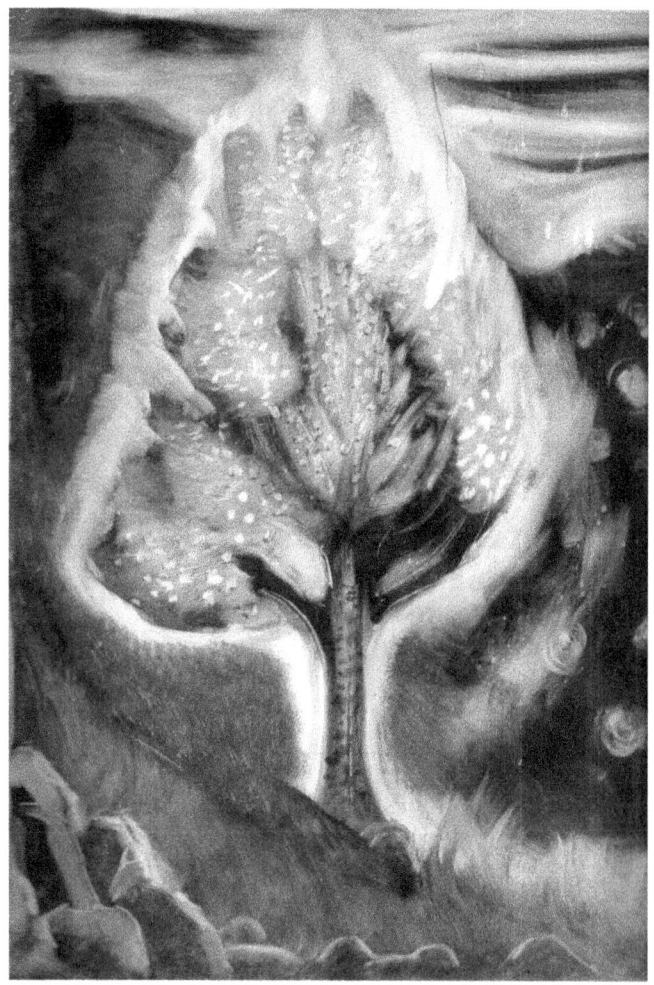

I travel on the wings of time and space,
Seeking out the spirit spots that listen
With a keening ear.
Their music echoed in my trembling
Delicate vibrations wavering
All tuned to worlds we cannot see

And have all but forgotten
In our quest for popularity.

The lone poplar
Growing old in good company and grace
Is I, is I, is I.

I court death wisely
Measuring man's time and space.
Benign bestower.
But who listens now?

Meditation

Imagine you are standing alone before a lone aspen on the mountainside. As you listen to the rustling of the leaves in the cool air, their sound guides you into a trance, where you feel totally present, totally part of the enchantment nature brings you. Spirit resides in the wind, and speaks through the aspen now for your benefit. It will bring you a sacred message. First you must search yourself for any fears you may have, or apprehension borne of fear. Feel your fears, and let them come to the surface as you gently breathe in and out.

Now pass your fears over to the aspen. She absorbs your fears willingly. Ask her now for help in conquering your fears in some problem area of your life. She places before you a blanket of dark air to cloak your fears. Take your fears out of your heart now and fill the blanket with these fears and return it to the aspen with gratitude. Perhaps you want to make a small gesture toward the tree to acknowledge her service to humanity, for she is a psychic shield for your fears. Now the tree sparkles with light and you notice it clearer than before. Your dark fears have illumined the aspen as she transforms them into the light. Move closer to the light that lies before you. It fills you with new energy now you have released your old worries.

Listen how every drooping branch shakes her fairy coins in every single breeze. The urgent whispering of the leaves affects your memory now, and you recognize your ancient self. As you sense who you originally were, the tree sparkles its light more.

There is a sacred message in the sound of the leaves for you. To help you hear it, try the following exercise.

Visualize a deep well. You are looking down into this well, and through the clear waters you notice a lot of sediment that is stirring up from the bottom. The sediment is created from all our unhandled emotions and karmic debt. These emotions slow our ability to achieve what we have come here for. You may feel despondent at times, or overwhelmed at your lack of achievement so far, or unable to discover what your purpose is. Let those feelings bubble up like the sediment rising in the well, and do not resist the movement. As it comes to the surface, know that it is going through a recycling process and will settle again, leaving you with new insights you can use to re-evaluate who you are, or what you saw or felt. Now thank the well for sharing its depths with you, and walk away with a spring in your step, for you know one day your body will pass away like everything in nature does, but your spirit never dies. Take your place now in the cycle of nature and feel free to be your true self.

You are becoming more present, more alive, and more eternal. Dusk sets in, and nature feels enchanting. You are part of nature, always supported by her. Relax and feel the unconditional love that nature brings. Acknowledge now that you are part of nature. There is no need to struggle so. Just go with the flow, like the aspen does, and you will feel freer to express yourself.

What do you want to express?

How can you express it in your own unique way?

Now is the time for you to achieve your soul purpose, by not resisting.

Affirmation
I am free to express my true self when I let go of false attachments.

Dance of The Year: A Series of Meditations

Yew Season – I – Idho (Winter)

I am as deep as darkness
I am as still as a seed in winter
I bestow beauty on shadow-
Illuminating depths.

In my silence,
I echo a primitive eternity.
I serve the seasons in my stillness.
I guard secrets to the world beyond

Come through my gate
And behold, beyond.

Meditation

Let us undergo a symbolic death as we journey with the yew. First of all, place yourself in a comfortable position and let your mind focus on your body. The yew will make anything that hinders you on your journey through life disappear now. You have no control over this final step for you agreed to come into this blessed planet when you were born, and you also agreed to return to the cosmos whence you came. The trees form an important part of the earth cosmos. We all ultimately are to work with the seasonal energies of the yew. So let all parts that hinder your progress melt under the spell of the yew.

To embody the process of the yew, feel for any parts of your body that do not resonate with vigour. Breathe streaming silver light into each part of your body that is weakened, or in pain. Believe as you breathe that you are sending healing light to the ligaments, the cells, the muscles and organs. As each breath enters your body, feel the old pattern cast off and leave you. Feel the lightness of being increase as you cast off any part that feels hindered from being free and mobile and full of life. Let all your conditions fall away. When you feel good, ask the yew for protection. Ask it now to show you an image for your spirit. Feel into the image you receive, whether it is a colour, a symbol, a happening or whatever in your mind's eye. Use the image to inspire you to express yourself, your spirit.

Come back into your body and focus on your body parts. If you feel sad or trapped in any way, concentrate on sending warm feelings into your body – love your body now, sending it light and warm colours. Send warm colours into your heart now. You can rest well after your struggles.

Affirmation

Resting in the earth, I enjoy the stillness and silence, for it frees my spirit more.

In the following energetic overview of the Celtic Year, let it soak in like a dance performed before your etheric eyes. When we look at the lunar trees, I am mainly looking at their inner qualities. I like to see it as examining the tree souls. These soul qualities manifest in physical ways too. The way a tree grows, the places it inhabits, the elements it can thrive under, all hint at the workings of its soul.

My primary source of inspiration for this book came from a poetry book I wrote in 1999. It was in turn inspired by the ancient manuscript by Taliesin: Battle of the Trees. I feel this battle poem illustrates how the Celts could expand their imagination into nature. Robert Graves too had studied the manuscript and gained great insights from doing so.

Spiritual scholar Eleanor Merry in her book *The Flaming Door: The Mission of the Celtic Folk Soul* studied the Celts from a spiritual perspective. She sensed that their elders bore a non-intellectual knowledge of the Christ consciousness. She wrote "They attained this knowledge through a natural clairvoyance, and their way had to go." What is Christ consciousness? The Christ consciousness functions as an embodiment of love that encompasses the All. I do not see it as a religious, but rather as a spiritual impulse in every living being. To reach a deeper understanding of the trees, I made a contract with myself. I wanted to touch the universal love, or Christ consciousness, that these trees store. By the end of one year I thus created a series of meditations on Celtic Trees.

Having introduced the vowels above, we now can consider the procession of the lunar months. Bear in mind that they are coloured by the moods of their relative seasons.

Dating of the Lunar Calendar

The dating of the yearly cycle of trees is based on the lunar cycles and over the years people have developed their own approaches for calculating these. Some base the start of each lunar month on the new moon and others on the full moon. I personally follow the new moon cycle that traces one whole lunar cycle. Some consider a lunar year to start at the festival of Samhain in early November, while others take the midwinter festival (Winter Solstice) as its starting point. I am inclined to take the latter approach because I like to imagine the return of the light begins a new cycle. In calculating the start of each lunar month I would take the first new moon after the Winter Solstice and follow the cycle of the moon until the next new moon. The year starts with the birch tree (Beth), so Beth begins on the first new moon after the Winter Solstice. In some solar years there are thirteen new moons; in others there will only be twelve.

I would ascribe the thirteenth lunar tree to a period leading up to the start of the Birch. It is an arbitrary period depending on how you sense it from year to year. The lunar year belongs to an entirely different mind-set to our solar year mind-set, which is more rational. Some people go to enormous lengths to calculate how the lunar months fit in with the twelve-month solar year. However, the thirteen rather than twelve months that belong to the lunar calendar is a mystical affair. Thirteen has always been a mystical number and I write about its symbolism later. Naturally thirteen lunar months will not be tied to fixed dates, and every nineteen years, more or less, the months return to a new cycle, coinciding with the solar dates that occurred at the start of the lunar nineteen year cycle. In our more linear world we modified this natural cycle so we can view the lunar cycle on a yearly basis within fixed solar dates. It is unnatural but it is a working model to hang our subtle feelings on. I feel it makes sense to view the Elder, the thirteenth month, as a brief time preceding the Birch tree. Below are the new moon dates for the lunar months for 2017 in Ireland.

1. Beth (Birch) December 29 to January 28
2. Luis (Rowan) January 28 to February 26
3. Nion (Ash) February 26 to March 28
4. Fearn (Alder) March 28 to April 26
5. Saille (Willow)/Straif (Blackthorn) April 26 to May 25
6. Huath (Hawthorn) May 25 to June 24
7. Duir (Oak) June 24 to July 23
8. Tinne (Holly) July 23 to August 21
9. Coll (Hazel)/Quert (Apple) August 21 to September 20
10. Muin (Mistletoe/Vine) September 20 to October 19
11. Gort (Ivy) October 19 to November 18
12. Ngetal (Broom/Reed) November 18 to December 18
13. Ruis (Elder) December 18 to January 17

You can see how the last month runs into the following year 2018. It means that for 2017 the Elder has only 13 days.

As you can see the lunar calendar is fluid with different dates for the lunar months each year. Therefore I would not ascribe fixed dates to the lunar months, but advise you to consult a yearly moon calendar to find the New

Moon dates for your area. However since the lunar months do not begin on January 1st, please accept that this is a hypothetical system that offers many seekers a valid spiritual model on which to base their inner journey from year to year. I myself will consult the lunar calendar to calculate which lunar tree essence to give a client. I will introduce the tree essences later in the book.

I first realized the intricate inter-connectivity between the lunar months and their respective seasons when a playwright had asked me for insights into St. Brigid as a figurehead for Irish wisdom. I instinctively examined the trees surrounding Imbolc, the festival associated with this deity. St. Brigid stems from the pagan goddess Bride or Brid. She represents an archetypal female energy that endures to this day. I saw that the lunar trees of the Birch, the Rowan, the Ash and the seasonal Elm all relate well to one another. (Incidentally there is an alternative tree for the Elm in some Celtic Tree calendars, which is the Pine. However, for simplicity I will only refer to the Elm.) The later legends of St. Brigid display many of their characteristics.

St. Brigid's Knees beneath ancient hawthorn on pilgrimage route in the Burren

I sensed how the legends arose from a collective soul of humanity. Legends help create a more permanent fixture in this universal soul that strives for freedom.

And so it was with St. Brigid that my meditations began. I sat on a cold mountain in the heart of the Burren in Ireland, contemplating two indentations in the rock where she knelt! A rough, cobbled pathway of stones was still visible. It led to an old gnarled hawthorn beside the rock. Known as St. Brigid's Tree and Brigid's Knees, legend has it that she knelt here to pray on her way from Galway. The traditional pilgrim walk on Imbolc or St. Brigid's Day had long ended. Nevertheless, the landowner respects the wishes of modern day pilgrims such as myself. On a very cold February morn, I crouched tentatively under the tree to shelter from the biting winds and boggy pasture. Stilling my slight irritation with the weather, sensations and visions filled my mind. After some while I felt I had enough inspiration to return home. There I completed the meditation, adding a final affirmation that seemed appropriate.

It is tempting to sit inside and imagine the tree, rather than venture out on dark, broody days. I found that if I did venture out, the memory of the journey helped me embody the qualities of the tree more. Of course I also could do a journey in my imagination to meet the spirit of the tree. This held a different quality though. I preferred to sit outside if at all possible.

When I look back over my body of tree-based knowledge, I can see a pattern emerging. The yearly cycle of trees seems to describe our own inner journey. It is a form of Grail quest for hidden knowledge, which ultimately is the knowledge of Self.

Birch – B – Beth

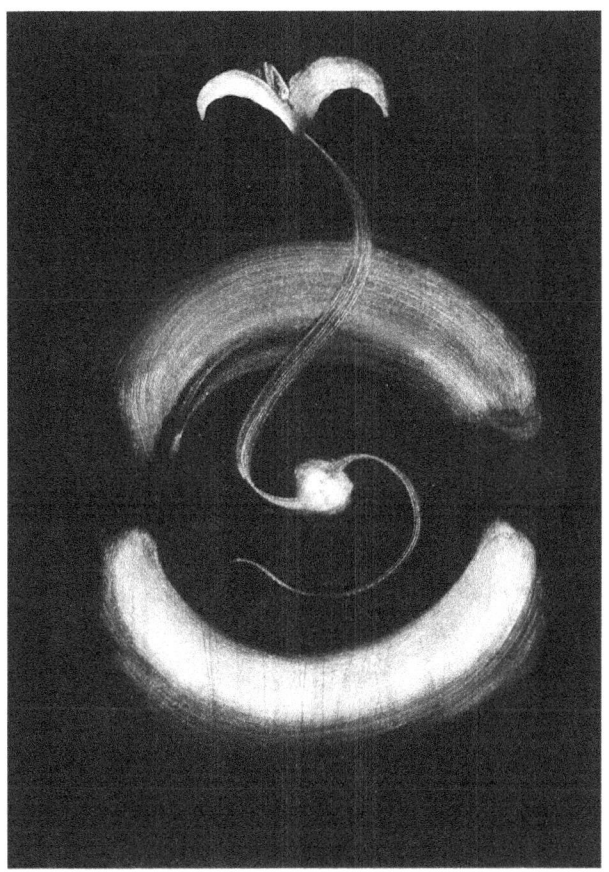

I grace the skies
With Slender forms
Embracing space
Like none other.

And Venus beckons me to her chamber
To rest my weary limbs

Against the greying skies.
She bathes me with all her love
And restores me.

I will give you life
Wherever you are
Whether you are
Alone or in company,
Near or far.

Why hesitate? I seem your bidding
At the beginning of the year.

Meditation

Know that your breath carries with it great life-giving forces. As you take a breath all the way from beneath your feet up into your heart, gather all the fire that you have stored so patiently over the last few months. Breathe out white light from your heart in all directions. Imagine the light is so bright it burns everything it touches. Keep breathing like this, feeling the healing of the fiery light you are releasing.

Now change to imagining you are breathing water from just below your feet. Let it pass through your body and leave through your crown. As it leaves your crown, it vapourizes and drifts skyward toward Venus. Breathe a blue light down again from Venus, letting it pass as vapour through your crown and down and out the soles of your feet into the earth where it condenses once more. Continue this two way flow of water into vapour into light for a while. Then focus on your heart. How does it feel to witness this courtship between Venus and Earth?

Now imagine you are a spirit of the Birch. You stand as a white goddess. Below your feet you feel a stream of silver light streaming into the womb of Mother Earth, like an umbilical cord. This connection makes your mind soar. It can penetrate any problem fast. Your spirit lifts at the ease with which your mind can focus now. You begin to dance in the clear orb of light that surrounds you. Your limbs are pliable and can withstand any storm. You are spreading such beauty through your vibrations that the whole world around you starts to sing. You truly are the Lady of the Woods. Everywhere you look, you feel an innocence that responds to you openly. A hare rushes by and you feel great empathy with it.

Affirmation
I shine my light stronger as I connect to the fiery interior of the Earth. Now I am filled with hope for my Life.

Rowan – L – Luis

I am the fire of effervescence
Solar-led
Beads of fire
Perspiring
In a fountain of release.

Light-illuminating spirals deflecting
Loss of wholeness.

> Protected, I lead you
> To your world of higher senses
> Preparing your descent again.
> Within, without, you turn.
> You mirror me, and grow
> Return, blessed and whole.

Meditation

Imagine you are a magical Tree of Life, bearing perpetual fruits at each cross quarterly and new moon throughout the year. Gather the heat of the Sun into your translucent body, and shine the light of the Moon from your luminous bark. As liquid fire seeps into your blood, your interior becomes deliciously warm. There is a great internal buzz as your forces of intuition rise. You feel strong and confident that you will be guided in all that life throws at you. Breathe the Sun into your heart for several minutes, building strength upon strength.

In your roots you remember the time of darkness now past. Thank the great dragon that has protected you and ask it to continue to protect you against all the residual spirits of darkness that may linger. You are ready to continue your journey onward to your home in the Sun. Brigid the Sun goddess loves your calm beauty and graceful energy, and she guides you to bring forth healing, strength and purpose. Now feel gratitude for your roots that protect the life forces. Simultaneously give thanks for your crown that protects the environment around you.

You have to release something into the underworld. Then something new can come in. Brigid appears. Her green resplendent gown shimmers and she bids you to release something from your roots. Let it be the first thing you see in your mind's eye. Do not question it. Has it left you? How does it feel after your act of release? Do you feel more present?

Imagine a stone circle somewhere. Your spirit is one with the rowan growing on the edge. You have chosen this spot because it is full of powerful earth energies. See the leys travel through the land the circle stands on. As the invisible forces of the earth rush through the circle, the rowan invites you to enter the tree. You can do this as you have an affinity with the earth dragons that live beneath the circle.

Let us journey to the home of one of these dragons.

Take a deep breath, and in spirit travel deep down into the bowels of the earth below the tree. You enter a large dark cavern that feels welcoming. As your eyes adjust, you see a small recess in the cave on which there is seated a beautiful creature sitting in a passive posture. As you start to gaze at it, the creature stirs and sits up with more vigour. It is a small dragon and its eyes look toward you. You see some fear or apprehension in its eyes. Through his eyes he communicates that he has to journey up to the surface, to visit some of the surface places. He has to follow a straight line. He fears whom he may encounter leaving the cavernous home. You know there is a reason for meeting him today. Now tell him about the rowan tree he will meet when he travels up. The tree will match his fire with her fire, and teach him many hidden mysteries of the earth. This knowledge will guard him well against any enemies. The dragon rushes on with new hope, and when he reaches the rowan in the human world, he listens well to what the rowan has to say. The rowan begins by telling him that she is protected by another, much larger, dragon. They each are intertwined by an energy that gives and receives the fire of protection. The dragon senses the great benevolence of the tree. He relaxes into a state of deep receptivity, and as he does, he sees the tree at one point shape-shift into a standing stone and back again. The power of the place is protected and anchored by the tree, but it could equally well be replaced with a stone programmed for protection. The dragon goes on its way with a light heart and steady tread, for it has lost his fear. Turn away now, knowing you will continue your journey through the year with a bright strong heart.

Imbolc is round the corner. You are already receiving the blessings of Brigid.

Affirmation
The dreams I nurture for this life will come to fruition.

Ash – N – Nion

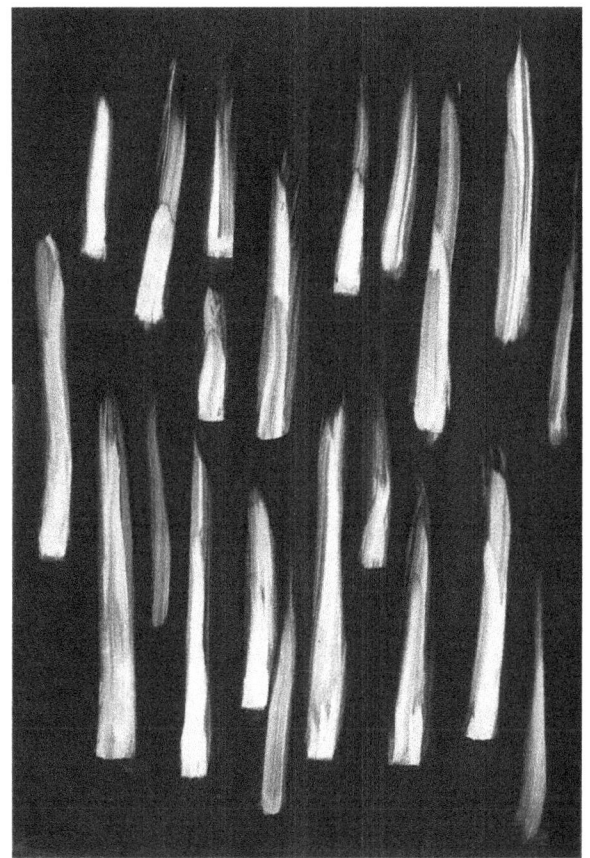

I eagle-eye the forest,
swoop and scoop the unrevealed
whilst soaring upward to the sun.
Beneath me my Mother the Earth
feeding me deep waters from her womb,

I am a spear thrust upwards
sap rising to my Father the Sun.

> My cry delves deep into brown veins
> "I am the spirit of survival!
> The spirit of Success.
> The flowing milk of the Season!"

Meditation

Imagine you are an ash - with your roots going deep into the ground, reaching far and sucking up the fluids. They rise as sap through your body, reaching your many arms that bend gracefully earthbound, and then gently arch upwards toward your crown. Your crown arches wide around your body, and it receives rays pouring from the Sun.

You feel the influence of the moon in your body fluids. Now get in touch with your emotions and if you detect any out of balance, release them as you breathe in and out. If you feel obsessed about someone or some situation, or even possessed a little by an energy you can't quite pinpoint, let it pass through your body and out. Now feel the energy of the Sun pour through your crown, filling you with a strong life force. How does it make you feel? Does it make you feel uneasy? When there is balance, you can feel joy. Just let in the force through your crown, down your trunk into the earth, and take up the lunar forces fed by the tree roots. Let these flow up through your veins. Let it flow in and out, up and down, without worrying how you are doing. Trust in a breathing process that will start to heal you, wherever it is needed.

Affirmation

We heal through embracing the male and female in harmony. Then we open to the many levels of our being in our time of transformation.

Alder – F – Fearn

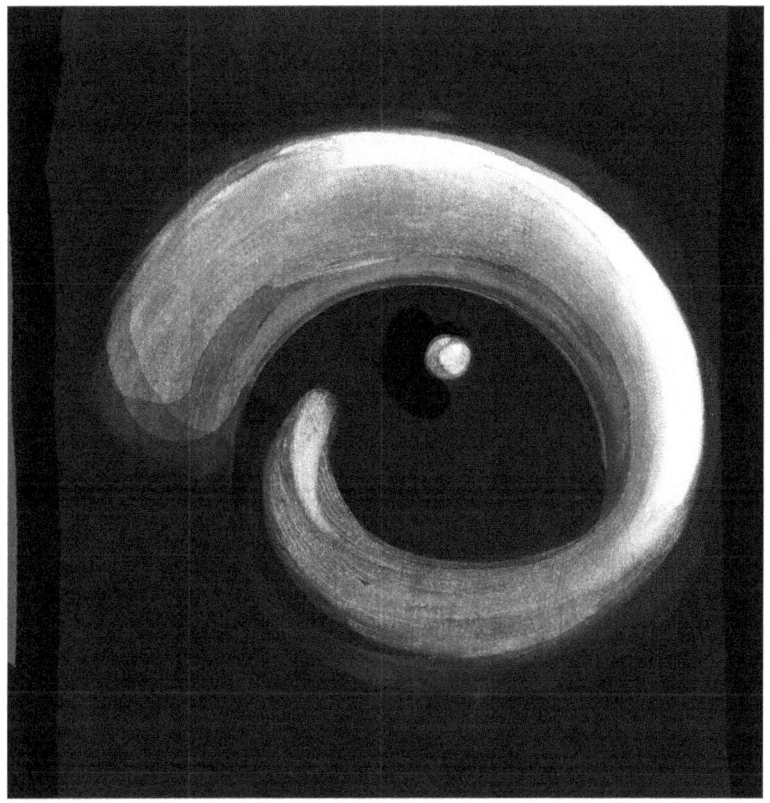

I come from the ancient lands
When water was abundant
and Knowledge too.

While my shape is shrouded in mystery,
my shield will still protect you -
unknown depths lurk.

Believe in my blessedness.
Respect my threshold.
Receive my smouldering fire.

I am the invisible spark
of inner will,
honouring the darkness still
in the need to fulfill
my destiny.

Some see a noble sacrifice
of strength -
but these deepest, darkest parts
cast in patient vigil
bear a flame invisible.

I seek you
in your hour
of greatest transformation
I await you still.

Meditation

Begin this meditation by tuning into your own personal space. Whatever has been going on around you in your life, withdraw now into your own safe space. Imagine you are under a shady alder, close to the healing waters that team with life. The alder protects all. Let your body relax by the water and breathe deeply. Observe your emotions now. How are you feeling? Once you have identified your emotions, imagine placing them in a thin membrane sack. Gently drop the sack into the water and watch the sack dissolve, diluting your emotions slowly until they just turn into liquid, dappled light. Continue to breathe. Stay with an empty mind.

The water laps against the branches and bark of the alder, which stands by the bank in serenity. The alder provides a foundation for your prayers. Ask for healing in all aspects of your life that require it. Centre yourself and focus on your heart. Venus is your guide now. Her healing affects every aspect of your being. Together with the ash, the alder holds the space for transformation. The alder can see into the future light, and carries a smouldering passion in his heart. Let your heart send healing light into the coming year, for you, and for all the world. The wood of the alder burns bright and slowly, and this is the type of healing it brings.

Affirmation

I am in this for the long run, and I allow love to be my guiding light. In doing so, I activate the divine will of God.

Willow – S – Saille (twinned with Blackthorn)

I carry the gentle mystery of hope
In the spaces I weave.
Leaning like tentacles
Eagerly clutching
Visions of the night
Brought back into the Light.

I hover on the edge of Dreamtime
Enveloping the Well of Water Divine.
No time for Death, nor yet for Life alone.

A sense of something else –
A surgeon carving stiches on your soul
So your fears drop
One by one.

> The journey completed
> Once embarked upon,
> Yet renewed
> Moment by moment.
>
> I dissipate pain.

Meditation

The willow tree energetically is aligned with the pause between our breaths. Before you start this meditation please bring your attention to your breath. Every moment of our lives, we breathe in and out. Take some time to observe your breathing, and as you breathe, we can focus now on the pause between the in-breath and the out-breath. Breathe out, and focus on the tiny pause at the end, before you breathe in again. Similarly, as you breathe in again, notice any pause at the end before you breathe out again. Now continue to breathe in this manner, bringing love and healing to the pause between your breaths. Without straining, you can allow the pause to extend itself a little, giving it some space. After a while this will become a habit. Remember, as you breathe in, pause a little, and as you breathe out, pause a little.

The pause is an obscure yet essential aspect of our breathing. It brings a sense of suspense to our breathing, which links to processes in both life and death.

The pause is the key moment in which we can reprogramme ourselves and re-ignite ourselves with new healing vibrations.

You are in your element within the gaps between the breaths, and in those gaps you become an aspect of cosmic love, fertile and healing. Absorb that love you can feel now in your heart.

Know that your day and your night are equal companions in your soul.

Spread the love into the clear light of the daytime of your soul, and let it fill you with a sense of harmony. And let love flood your mind, and let it fill you with strength in the night time of your soul. Between your heart and your mind, the light and the dark, you are in balance, a balance between the breaths. You carry the impressions of the day into your sleep. You dream in those moments, and carry the essence of each dream into your waking moments. Return to paying attention to your breathing. In the gap between your breaths, you can see clearly past the shadows, those shadows that once led you into darkness that betrayed. Imagine now you have found a way to let your shadow illuminate your path by working with your dreams.

In willow time, you are invited to delve into the deep waters of your soul. Take a while now to imagine yourself standing in a moonlit swamp. Imagine you are a willow, with your roots held fast in the magical swamp. The slow-moving waters fill your presence with a neutral stance of observation. You call on the moon to bring the rains, the love, the healing, and mystery of living. Butterflies and bees love you, for you exude great love, and great healing. The moonlight is rippling on the waters below, concealed in the undergrowth that surrounds you. You can stand swaying in the night breeze, and embrace the rays of the moon, absorbing her light and sending it far into your limbs and bark. Let your watery body dance into ecstasy with the liquid crystal moon above. You feel great love and peace and harmony while you dance in subtle moves. As you stand swaying, allow the dreamtime you know so well to teach you her messages. Death is not your memory, for you have an aspect of a higher reality in your veins that connects you with the beyond. Be still, and know that in that stillness is the greatest movement of all, for anything can be achieved in this gentle quality of balance and harmony.

Affirmation
When I am still, it is then that I know I am strong.

Dance of The Year: A Series of Meditations

Blackthorn – SS – Straif (twinned with Willow)

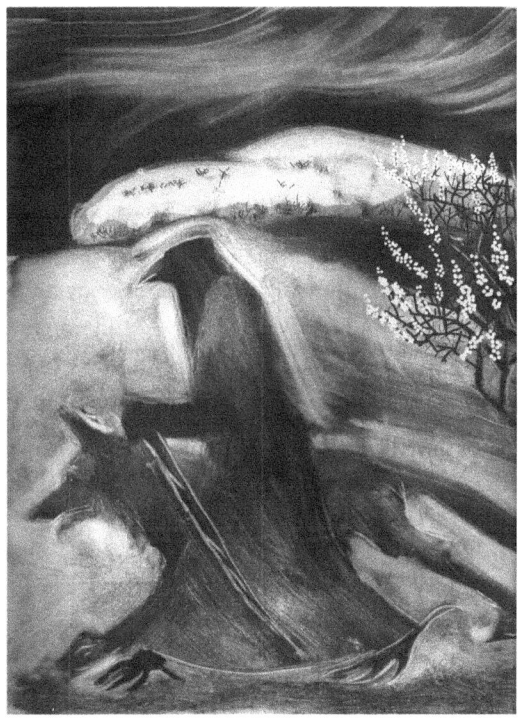

I conjure up my purgative fumes
And then
I stoke the flames
Inverting flames
Of molten inner states
Into a most stubborn fire.

Wielding the Old Hag
Upon the Innocent
And yielding fruits
Of the unfathomable.

Meditation
Try repeating the breathing exercise we used in the Willow meditation, and in the pause between the breaths invite the energy of the shape-shifting Old Hag to enter. Breathe in and pause, and then breathe out and pause, time and time again.

Imagine you are walking down a pathway in a thick forest, and you meet some old trees that have fallen across your path. You must get past them before nightfall, and you may wish to call upon some magical being to help you get past them more efficiently. It would be easy if you could just fly over them but you are trapped in your physical body and so you need an ally. Reach toward the ground between your feet, and notice there is a hilt of a sword gleaming at the level of the ground. Pull on this sword now. It rises slowly from the earth, still quite warm from being fashioned in the core of the earth. Grasp it with both hands, and feel the quality of truth that this sword is offering. Now feeling fearless with your sword of truth in hand, you sense that there is no need to follow the main path through the forest. Your path is one you alone create, and you see a way ahead through the dark forest. Younger trees grow here too, whose parents have fallen across the main path. The sword obeys your will, while your heart lies still, unquestioning as you move like a snake, winding your way, using your sword to merely touch young trees, that fall effortlessly to the ground when you move decisively forward. Whatever you touch with your sword falls away instantly. How many times must you pass through such forests? How many young trees must your sword glance before the final transformation? You are not counting, for you are completely in the rhythm of swinging your sword. You reach the end of the forest, where the sword at your side turns into a gleaming white sword. This is your sword of white truth and protection and might.

As you stop in your tracks, you shift dimensions and slip into the form of a blackthorn tree. Feel the energy of this ancient true warrior tree. Beneath his hard exterior, there always was love at the core. Now all external wars have turned inward to heal the perpetrators and the victims. You are tapping into an ancient creativity that is long overlooked. Embrace its essence so the imbalance can be addressed.

Now imagine you are holding your sword of truth, fully fashioned. You are the perfect male consort for the hawthorn who awaits you next month.

You have prepared the space for your sister well. For this you needed solitude, with few companions at your side. In your solitude, you learnt more than when you were active in the world.

The guided meditation you just did is very important for the times we live in, when we are witnessing so much of our physical world disintegrating. We all need an inner strength to proceed, without any attachment to the result.

In these times there is no place for negativity. We need to cultivate the inner strength to overcome our outworn patterns. So the guided meditation was also about cutting out all negative thoughts that are the source of real pain. The young trees represent the rebirth of your negative thought patterns when they appear across your pathway. You eliminate those thoughts with grace not aggression. Embrace the times when you trip up, when you find yourself falling into old patterns, for with patience and willpower you can overcome everything. You will find the power in you to co-create the new Christ energy so we can wake up to a new world in the future.

Affirmation
I appreciate the grace my shadow bestows upon me.

Hawthorn – H – Huath

I am the feminine
With fire so strong
That I remain;
Untouched
Unadulterated
At one with the Divas -
But not with men
Who long for me.

My celibacy celebrated in sun-kissed berries later in the season
Honour me, and I will protect you.

> My affinities are almost boundless,
>
> I am of the alluring wild –
> And not of garden kind.

Meditation

Settle yourselves comfortably and imagine you are a hawthorn standing in the centre of a fresh green field. Many spring flowers grow below your twisted boughs. You spread your limbs close to the ground, sensing and communing with the inner fire in the earth. Your heart rejoices in the fertility of the earth that has brought these flowers to your feet. You sing with a generous heart as you hear the cuckoo calling. As the cuckoo tree, your blossoms cluster so densely they shroud you in a cloud of white, for you have brought the dark of winter into the full light of summer now. And every day you bring the moonlight of the previous night into the day, reflecting it in your white mantle. Your cloak of blossoms whisper of the thin veil that exists between two worlds you inhabit with ease. The fairy and the human world intertwine here. While you stand guard in the field, you bring a fierce sense of fiery presence. Such is the complexity of your sweet apparel, which cloaks a female warrior.

Now step aside of your tree form and become your human form again. Look back at the hawthorn standing there, and reach with your arms around the tree, gathering creamy white flowers to your bosom where you feel their warmth. You stoop to pick daisies and buttercups that you enjoy weaving into a garland, and then you place your floral crown upon a high branch in the tree. Wait now and watch or feel the fairies appear shyly to dance around the branch adorned with yellow flowers you have picked for them. The fairies appreciate your gesture for it shows respect for their especially beloved tree. Now they show you the spirit of elemental love rising within the tree, and they extend that love to you so you too are protected from evil spirits. They invite you to open any emotions that have been building up inside you, and let them burst forth. The fairies will take your bottled emotions away, and purify them in the fairy space that surrounds the hawthorn. Watch how the spirit of pure love rises within the tree again, purifying, strengthening, flowing freely. Pay attention to the spines of the trees, where the fairies store their magic. As your gaze returns to the whole tree, see how it has become a flame of pure love in the world, casting its heady aroma all around, so the union of god and goddess, Sun and Moon, Fairy King and Queen, can begin.

Finally, let's enter the spirit of the hawthorn, which is essentially a loving, happy tree. Remember that you can create your own happiness, by imagining the feelings. Breathe in deeply and drink in pure light, pure love. Let it fill your heart again and again as you take deep breaths in and out. Again, breathe in pure light, pure love and let it enter your heart, and bathe your heart with positivity. In the next breath in, let the love enter your heart and focus on its tenderness.

Once you feel that these feelings have filled you to capacity, let happy thoughts enter on the in-breath.

Let the thoughts fill your mind and even let them fill your head with dizzy happiness. Concentrate on bringing in happy thoughts as you breathe in and out now.

Finally breathe in warm rays of the sun. Relax and know that all is love in the end.

Affirmation
I seek and enjoy happy thoughts that dwell in the protective pulse of nature.

Oak – D – Duir

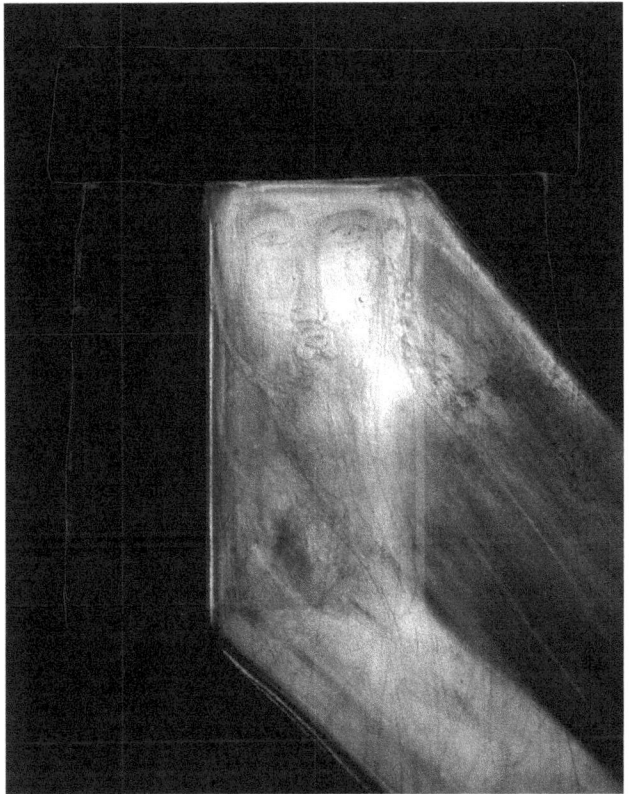

I am the Sun Warrior triumphant
Standing guard to the aeons,

Protecting
Earth with my eternal oath.

In between the crack
There am I –
The sun warrior triumphant
Standing steadfast at the door.

> I, protector of the Earth
> Gathering forces in untouched realms
> Undeterred by creatures of linear time,
> In a constant state of expectancy.
>
> The initiated recognize
> My presence.
> The uninitiated share the awe.
>
> My seed
> Waits patiently,
> Forever ripening.
> Solemnly toasting
> The future kingdom.

The future kingdom is upon us now. The oak carries the collective efforts and qualities of the previous trees to fruition in an act of almost effortless courage now.

Meditation

To find this courage, start working with your breath, breathing in and out and connecting on each breath to the earth below your feet. Pay attention to the plantar area of your sole, for this is where the solar plexus of your body touches the ground. By breathing in and out through the ball of your foot, you can build up the energy in your solar plexus centre. Breathe light from the earth into your foot, and let it travel as far as your solar plexus before you then release your breath as light into the earth again. Continue to breathe like this for several breaths. Let that light build up in you and enjoy its strengthening aspect. Remember to return it to the earth again and again.

Imagine now the sun light above you in the sky, and feel connected to its wonderful warmth. Call in this physical sunlight. It is a raw energy such as you may have sensed as a child. Bring in the light now and let it travel down to your heart chakra, where it starts to form a sun child. As you breathe out, let the energy of that sun child pass down to your feet and continue through them into the earth. Know in each breath that you are carrying the sun child into the earth where it becomes the seed of a new earth child, illumined and unique. As you carry the energy back up to your heart to repeat the cycle, you are assisting a new sun being about to incarnate. You feel free and fearless. Your pillar of light is very strong now. You have become a gentle giant, connected to the earth and carrying the seed of a new earth child within you.

When you have made a firm connection from your heart to above and below, feel how it forms a pillar of light inside your body. When you are ready, on your next out-breath spread your light laterally from your heart, so that you create a cross of light from your heart. As you continue to breathe, with each breath imagine inspiration is entering you.

Ask for inspiration as you breathe and note what comes to you. The oak is the incarnater of ideas, so stay with the process until you are satisfied you have connected to the oak energy that is prevalent now.

Affirmation
I stand as endless potential, connected to all in love.

Holly – T – Tinnhe

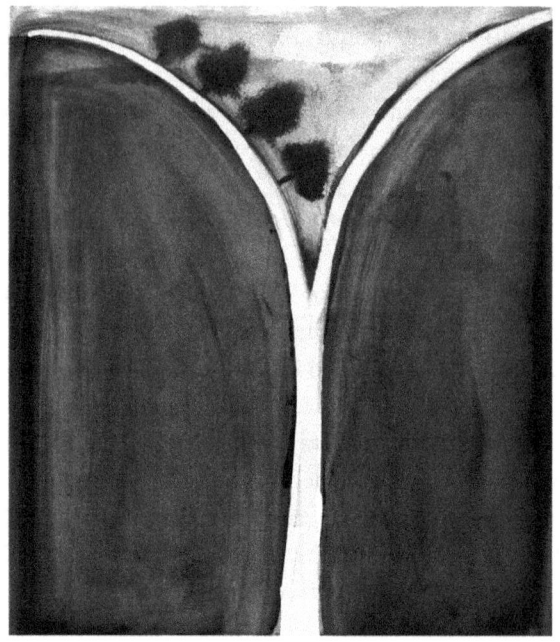

I am the king who heralds in
All that is good and wholesome.
And indeed holy.

My iron splendid
Adorns the space
I viscously defend

I grow old and tough
The very stuff
Of the fluid victorious.

Pass me by, and hearken to my blessing
Use if for universal good.

Dance of The Year: A Series of Meditations

Meditation

Begin breathing in and out. Send each breath you exhale all the way down to your feet and through the balls of your feet. Pay attention to the balls, for it is here where your feet touch the ground. You may imagine a buzzing area just below the soles in the middle of your feet as you keep breathing in and then sending the out-breath downwards. Breathe in again and send the energy back up as far as your solar plexus. Continue doing this for a few minutes. You may pause the recording to practise this for a while. Then continue with the next stage.

Now we are going to add colour to your breath. As you breathe out, send a blue ray down into the earth, and on each in-breath direct a golden ray upwards as far as your solar plexus on your body.

You may pause to practise this for a while. Then continue with the next stage.

Imagine that your body is standing in a core of golden blue light. As you continue breathing, expand that core so it becomes a solid beam or column of light surrounding you.

Now look into the column from outside of yourself, sending loving thoughts to yourself, bathing in that pale golden blue hue. Remember to keep breathing, and send a fiery red energy towards that column now. So it becomes a violet/golden hue as the colours all mix together.

Look for anything stirring within the new light. Savour the images.

The violet light belongs to the holly. It is most holy and it does not show itself so readily, so you have to imagine it into existence.

Now imagine this light as a soft metal. Imagine it as a soft rod of iron. Keep breathing and as your breaths flow on, let that metal harden more, and its top become a spear pointing to the heavens.

Return to your body now standing within the violet rod. There is pure light pouring from the tip above you. Turn yourself so the tip points towards an area of darkness outside you. Release your light. How does it feel? Remain with that feeling, breathing a while longer.

Affirmation

I grow exponentially by working with the mystery of the cosmic forces of Gaia.

Hazel – C – Coll (twinned with Apple)

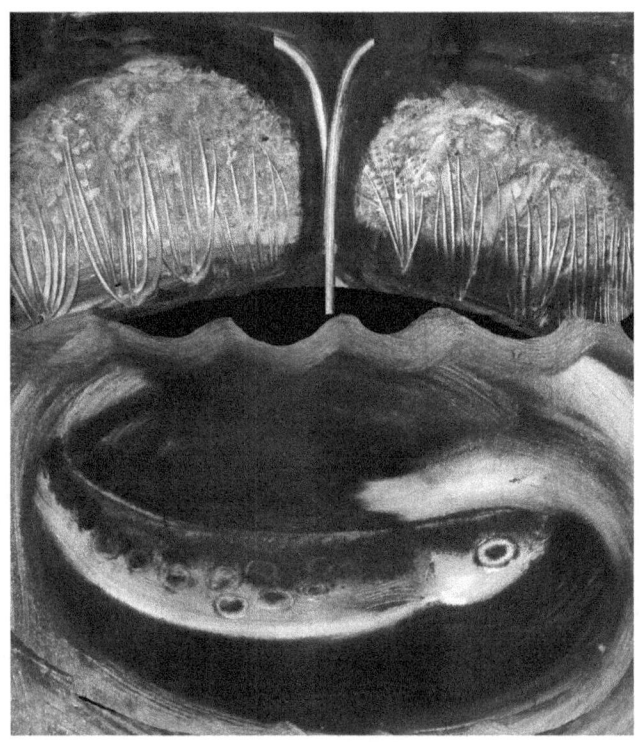

I wave my wand with fairer face,
Mine is a noble grace.
I impart wisdom
And cast light on the shadows
With my enduring powers.

I long to show
My treasures.
But only those who approach
With due care
Can commune
With my treasures

Dance of The Year: A Series of Meditations

Bound beyond
The shimmering sheen
Of diamond pinnacles
Sky-bound
Beyond the silver waters
Of deepest wells earthbound.

I satisfy and end your search,
Your thirst, your hunger
And potentize your memory.

Meditation

Imagine you are holding rods of hazel in your hands. They protect you and boost your powers of intuition. Breathe naturally, and as you breathe in and out, imagine each cycle bringing you closer to the higher truth that lies hidden from everyday routines. Your breath takes you inside where there is positive light shining for your soul to delight in. Outwardly your body remains quite still. Inwardly your soul is travelling fast through hidden capillaries and channels, toward a rich tapestry of light.

Take some time to imagine this process of every cycle of breath becoming a journey toward the light. Savour the pure light and the beautiful patterns that it creates.

Reach with your hands into that light and pluck a ball of light from the field of light you see in your mind's eye. Let that ball of light roll into your heart, and ask the question "What is it I need to know right now?"

Listen to any wisdom that is shown to you. This is knowledge you need to continue your journey with. When you have heard sufficient, or feel satiated, imagine the light from your heart spread throughout your body and surrounds, and at the same time let the ball of light in your heart return to whence it came. Give thanks for its gift, for your newly acquired knowledge and wisdom is imprinted on the ball, and the light shines brighter with your essence.

Affirmation

I find the deepest treasures within when I surrender to the waters of the dreamtime.

Apple – CC – Quert (twinned with Hazel)

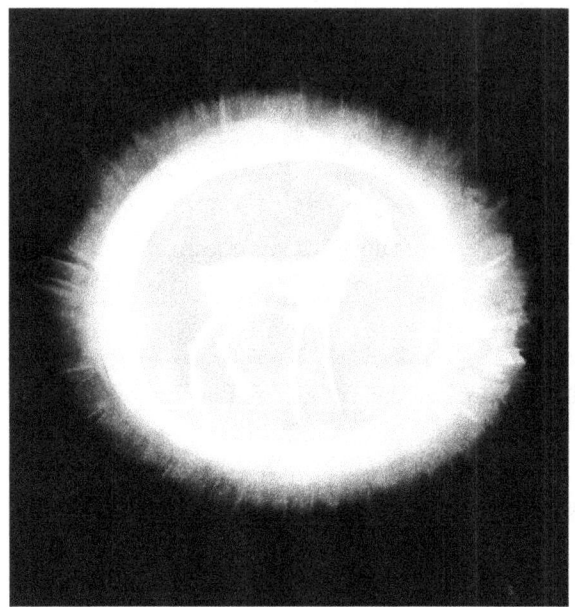

I dwell within the inner core
Weaving the dreams
That see and feel the seasons

Form an endless world.
With your heart
You hear me speak
A whisper rare
That bids you
Taste the fruit.

Few of you
Can pluck my fruit.
Few of you
Will dare.

> My gift to you
> Is rejected 'til
> My wondrous
> Wilderness
> Enters
> And leaves you
> In deep peace
> Through and through.

Meditation

The answers you received in your hazel meditation have brought you inner harmony that leads onto outer harmony sooner or later. Now let's dwell a while in the earth wisdom and magic of these dual trees. Return to the light of the hazel meditation. Start breathing in and out again, calling upon the apple tree this time. As you breathe your cycles of breath understand that this light is really the eternal light to which you return when you die. Dying is no everyday business and the apple tree affords you space here to imagine the spiritual beings that accompany you at death. Continue breathing, and imagine going toward the light. Part of your breathing is no longer your own: it belongs to the eternal spirit that all life shares. As you breathe, imagine the Great Spirit is accompanying your breaths and let it be. Do not resist. You are of the earth, but deeply connected to the heavens within the earth. See the light grow large, and reach out to pluck a light-filled apple from the ether, and let it sit comfortably in your heart space. Inside the apple lies a five-pointed star filling you with love and light. Feel it energize your heart, and sense a quality of paradise that the apple brings with it. This apple emits pure love and acceptance. It is whispering to you how you are dearly loved, as indeed you are. How could this cosmic light not love you for it created you as an expression of itself? Rest a while in the light of self-acceptance and love.

Affirmation

In truth I am eternal spirit filled with love and harmony for all.

Mistletoe/Vine – M – Muin

Berries of the Mistletoe
Airborne sperm.
Oh hidden tree of chieftains!
Divine equalizer mid-air

Clinging in rapture to
Hawthorn, ash and oak occasional
And above all the goddess tree.

The apple's High Branch
Plant of Al Heal, of peace
Emissary of the Sun,

Dangling to earth
Rendering her spirit fertile.

Dance of The Year: A Series of Meditations

Meditation

Start by paying attention to your breath, and as you breathe in from above take in creamy white light, almost like vapour, into your crown. Let the elixir of the mistletoe berries infuse your body and surround your body too in a cloud of healing light. Let the light flood your heart until it is fit to burst, and as you breathe out see the light spread around your veins, and let the cloud of light seep into the earth around your feet. After a few breaths like this shift your in-breath to golden light from the sun, filling you and surrounding you with warmth and vitality. As it reaches your heart, feel it bringing you a deep sense of peace and utter stillness. Remain one with the nothingness lying at your core. Open your eyes.

How do you feel?

Affirmation:

My roots lie in totally trusting the divine to provide me with all I need to grow.

Ivy – G – Gort

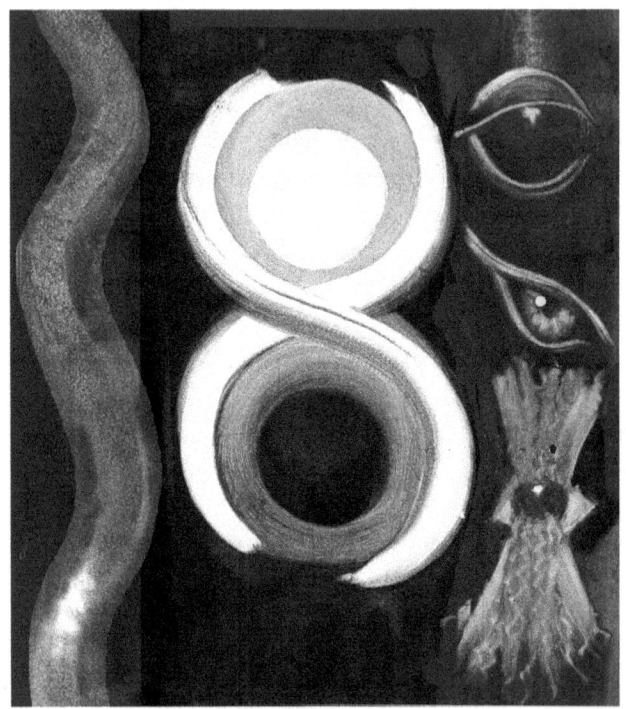

I offer you only frenzied glimpses
Of what lies between
One world and another.

Spiralling a web of dreams
The green goddess knows
Which are her own.

My one eternal breath
Feeds your yearning
And spins the turning
Resurrecting of your soul.

Meditation

Start to breathe in and out mindfully. Imagine a new moon on each in-breath and a full moon on each out-breath. The cycles of the moon create our Celtic Tree year, and a steady flow between the months depends on the archetypal hidden ivy. As Autumn approaches, the ivy becomes more visible as other growth decays. At this time of year, with the help of the ivy, you can overcome all odds. Your sharp wit is balanced by other female attributes: compassion and loyalty.

Close your eyes. Now let us go on a journey, across a land that is alien to you. You know nothing about the terrain and soon you find yourself caught out in a storm. Shortly, you meet an ugly green monster with a very pointed chin. Greet her with the words: "I accept you for I know that by accepting you as you are, you bring me gifts of real growth."

Perhaps you can think of a situation in your life that appears difficult right now. Replace the statement with that situation in mind: "I accept this situation for I know that by accepting this situation as it is, it brings me gifts of real growth".

Breathe naturally and feel this acceptance seep into your bones.

Return to your green-headed monster and now say: "I see you are turning into something new and quite beautiful".

See what your imagination transforms the monster into. Now think about your own apparently difficult situation. How does it make you feel? Then ask yourself what your true spiritual beliefs are. Persevere in this thought, and feel for a certain space that enters your feelings as you ponder your true beliefs. When you feel that space open up, know that you are in touch with beliefs that carry positive energy with them and will transform your current situation if you desire resolution. Continue with the exercise for however long it takes, within reason!

This opening of space may have a soft appearance to it. It brings you a certain charm and charisma that guarantees you certain survival through the current stormy situation you perceive.

Affirmation

I am deeply spiritual in unconventional ways.

Reed – R – Ngetal

Royal Veins
Silt-fed

Set me apart
As noble
And upright.

Meditation

In your imagination, look down upon the reed, and let your gaze reach into the brown silt that feeds its growth, and feel gratitude for all that has passed. Your gratitude is the key to setting you free. The next step offers you insight into your higher truth. This is the moment for desiring truth above all. The truth lies shuffled and compressed in the layers of silt beneath your feet. Select your personal question and send it to the all-knowing Spirit of the Earth each time you breathe out through the soles of your feet. Your question can ask about something related to your truth, what you need to know about yourself. Wait patiently for the truth to appear. Record what is revealed.

Imagine the reeds rising straight and noble from the silts of time on the fringes of a lake. Imagine you are standing peacefully beside the reeds, enjoying the respite that the scene offers. All is calm; all is cool. Ripples on the lake reflect images of reeds waving gently in their upright stances. As you gaze into the shadowy waters on the lake edge, understand that the reed is the keeper of records in the cycle of time. It retains the archives of your life to date that it imprints upon your soul. As you imbibe the essence of the Reed, you grow ready to take flight into the unknown when your time to go arrives.

Affirmation

I enjoy being firm and upright, thanks to lessons learnt from my past struggles.

Elder – R – Ruis

I oversee the cauldron
Surrounded by my good folk
Who love,
And court, the night.

I withstand decay wrought upon
My long suffering earth.
I await my transformation
From Old Hag into young maiden
Yet again.
Death cannot be delayed.
Embrace it tenderly,
For I remain
To guard your spirit,
Wrapping you sweetly
In my warm embrace.

Dance of The Year: A Series of Meditations

Meditation
Now you are freer than ever before. Breathe freely and enjoy this feeling of inner freedom. As you breathe in, imagine a strong white light reaching into you from the bowels of the earth, and let it rise through your core beam that travels the length of your spine. Let the light spread into your whole being, and as it rises it exits your crown and starts to arch and bend downwards towards its source, its mother the Earth. It enters the earth again and reaches into the primeval depths of the planet. There is wisdom of the ages stored there. Many beings of light create these beams of light from the energy gathered here. Give a gift to the light beings that protect this region. Now ascend through the earth towards its surface once more, and know that you are passing through a band of memory. It is the memory of the past year. The memory is active and creating a rich decomposing of events, seen as a swirl of brown and dark green light. Among the swirls you can see a spark of pure white light. Focus on this light and watch it grow rapidly, forcing its way to the surface as a clear band of regenerative white light that now passes through your body. It leaves little fertile beads of light in your belly. These seeds carry the potential for the New Year to follow. The light continues up your body and through your crown, only to descend again, leaving in its wake a brilliant arch of white light. Follow this light on its journey and witness how it makes a series of white arches across the land. Let your spirit enjoy a ride as you travel with this light, a light that protects you and starts to speak thus:

"I am the bridge between the old year and the New Year.

I am the bridge between the human and the fairy realms.

I am the bridge between all sets of twelve.

My light is alchemical. It is more absolute than the light of your world, and I transform all that is rotting into a new eager energy.

Feel my light envelope you. Bathe in my aura. Are you seeking wisdom? My light can grant you wisdom above all. I don't give it away lightly. I bid you name your intent for the New Year."

So take a few minutes and decide upon your intent. Then address the beam of light and state your intent as clearly as possible. As you state your intent, imagine your own aura of light spreading. How does it feel? What you have to realize here is that the purer your intent, the brighter and larger your aura will become and the more likely will the Elder embrace you in return with her light-filled energy. Allow her light to mingle with your own, so she may protect you and grant you prosperity, health and positivity for the New Year.

She exudes the love of Venus. Venus now calls from another tree the Oak, whose strong presence comes into view. The oak presents himself channelling her energy:

"I am of the Venus ray too and occupy the Overworld wherein humans mostly dwell. Here we are concerned with all matters physical, but I need and acknowledge your occupancy in the Underworld, where fairies and dryads dwell in the main. And so, from the opposite side of the lunar cycle, I am here to remind you that yin and yang must co-exist. I stand, a single Venus pole, to support my twin sisters the Elder that ends the year, and the Birch that begins the New Year."

And so, as your light re-enters the earth, breathe in and out all your love for Mother Earth, for her gifts of fertility, protection and all that is good and wholesome. Remain with your breathing, focusing on thoughts of gratitude for her bountiful self.

Send her your love from your heart. Let that heart expand in loving wisdom toward your fellow creatures. Send energy from your heart toward the Elder. What do you sense in return? Perhaps you see images. What images do you see? Pay her respect, and care for her core being and she will bless you in return.

Affirmation

When I can accept and love my shadows without guilt or shame or self-loathing, I can renew myself from my unfathomable depths.

Chapter 4

FLOW OF THE YEAR

TREES WHOSE NAMES START WITH vowels provide the structure for the lunar trees whose names start with consonants. Vowels represent a purer feeling uttered by our breaths. They are not created from the more mental constructs of consonants. We will briefly look at these vowels to see how they help shape the calendar with their distinguishable attributes. The vowels form the seasons that influence the consonants greatly, lending their distinct moods as follows.

Seasons

Elm AILM (Early Spring) New life after death
(Ruled by Planets Mercury and Saturn and the Element of Water.)
The elm offers a gentle and supportive start to the cycle of the Celtic Tree year. They are mythically associated with death although they belong to early Spring. Interestingly elms have long been linked to elves, which were believed to work with the spirits of the dead. The elfin connection remains, for the elves work with the wisdom of the earth to which the elm belongs. In plant medicine the elm is used to assist us contact spirits of various herbs. Today we can still see elms until about their thirty-first year, when ironically they die. They would generate an underground canopy of much needed nutrients for the soil if they were to spread successfully — a Dutch disease-bearing ambrosia beetle wiped out stocks in 1919. Hence the name Dutch Elm disease. A more virulent strain of the disease returned

to Britain in 1967. The trees once grew prolifically in Britain and Ireland. Often shaped like lofty ladies, they could reach as tall as 150 feet. Their reproduction methods have evolved into growing new saplings from their roots. The ash tree belongs to this same season. It too is suffering from a dieback disease, which threatens its extinction in Britain and Ireland. We are at the threshold of a new consciousness now, and nature too is turning. Every living thing is interconnected in an invisible stream of consciousness, and the large number of trees dying in this portion of the Celtic calendar suggests a response to the new energies on a more subtle level. Yet, let us remember that with death comes new life.

Elm trees help protect humans against lightning. Their branches were used for beating the bounds (marking the perimeter of a settlement) in ancient ceremonies, and were also used for divination purposes, and a whole host of superstitious activities.

At times the elm was called the Tree of Destiny. This hints again at the threshold that its lunar month the rowan guards. Others saw it as the Tree of Life in the Garden of Eden, closely linked to the Norse Tree of Life that its lunar ash tree represented. Whilst bound to the Earth, the elm has stillness, purity, love, light and wisdom that we forget at our peril. The graceful, almost vanished forms remind us of their feminine attributes. The wych elm is a smaller type of elm that grows by water. It is more common than the ordinary elm nowadays. There is a gentle stillness to the elm. The challenge here is to carry an awareness of our immortality even while we strive to incarnate. This awareness modulates the incoming fire of the next season, and allows the spirits of various realms to support us.

Gorse ONN (Late Spring/Low Summer) Progress in Adversity

(Ruled by our Sun and the Planet Mercury and the Element of Fire.)

The gorse is like the inspiring Sun warrior – bringing vigour, success and profusion. However, the battle is no longer about blood and gore, but about an etheric battle that dangles the possibility of great inner victories. This theme of inner drama continues throughout the tree cycle. Here we encounter the confident warrior who has incarnated and progressed by preparing inwardly, with the help of his lunar tree consorts the Willow and the Blackthorn.

The battle has begun. There is no turning back. This is the time to declare "In God I place my trust!" the motto of the Sinclairs of Scotland who adopted the Gorse tree as their totem.

Heather URA (High Summer) Passion, Love
(Ruled by Planet Venus and the Element of Water.)

The heather restores the battle-weary. She is the keeper of secrets. In this season a succession of lunar trees appear that are deeply intertwined with the devic world. The holly, hazel and apple trees are all concerned with the dreamtime, from which we bring back the gifts of intuition, healing, and inspiration. As humans we often access these other realms in our dreams. In these times, we can dream much into manifestation.

A word of warning; since the heather emits much heat and passion we have to temper that heat. Now is the time when we naturally lean toward intimacy with our fellow human beings, for the sun is high overhead making for long days and sunshine in which our bodies can relax. Ultimately we seek intimacy with ourselves to sustain us through the long winter on the other side of the year. Without balancing our outer activities with time to reflect and be still, we will become exhausted and over-stimulated. Let us maintain an inner connection to source that brings joy and contentment in its wake. Burnout is borne of disconnection. The devic beings that surround the heather are nurturing us now in the pulse of their home. They are encouraging us to relax, be inspired and create later.

Aspen EADHA (Autumn) Linked to the shadow, unknown
(Ruled by Planet Mercury and the Element of Air.)

The aspen aids regeneration. It offers a window into our soul. It can be seen as aiding a process of spiritual rebirth. Her strength helps us face the unknown by encouraging us to remain flexible and self-reliant, despite the blows that life throws at us from time to time. As our life progresses the opportunities for growth become more subtle, for we have to stand on our own two feet, and in many ways, we have to become our own angels, learning methods of self support. We may start cultivating an interest in the deeper earth dimensions. The aspen mediates for humans wishing to gain access to fairy realms.

The aspen's branches billow in ceaseless sway, driven by mercurial gusts of wind. As the dainty heart-shaped leaves quiver in fresh Autumn winds, they can remind us of the turning of the seasons, and the inevitable death that comes to us all.

The leaves are semi-translucent and allow the wind to pass through them easily, and the branches allow the wind to pass through with ease, and the tree survives the storms. This is a key to what this tree offers your soul.

Yew IDHO (Winter) Beyond life - Guarded threshold to rebirth
(Ruled by Planets Saturn and Pluto and the Elements of Earth and Water.)

The yew stands at the threshold between inevitable death and new life, looking back to the past and forward to the future. It reminds us of the wisdom we have accrued, and renews us with spiritual strength for what lies ahead.

The yew has a finality to it that could depress us unless we fully realize its other aspect: spiritual regeneration. The aspen season that preceded the yew season toughened us up and showed us our inner gifts. Now we can distill our unique qualities and express our essential natures with ease.

Months

Birch BETH

The birch lies between the yew (winter/death) and elm (spring/new life) seasons in midwinter. She represents new beginnings. Love is the foundation of all matter created. Birch is ruled by the Planet Venus and so links with fertility and love. In Irish mythology the birch offers lovers a trysting place. In this case of romantic love, we meet respectively in Diarmid and Grainne an immortal and ultimately mortal soul. They meet in a birch grove. This is fitting because the year is but beginning, and the human soul has not quite incarnated. Grainne is half immortal still at this stage.

After the darkness of decomposition there is the blessing of increase. After passing through the cauldron of rebirth overseen by the Elder at the beginning of winter, the Birch moves through midwinter to the time of Return of the Sun. The dark secrets of the underworld have transformed her Yin fire into Yang fire. As a Universal Woman, she can propagate life anywhere. Like the preceding Elder, Venus is her guiding Planet.

Birch brings a sense of self-healing and strength. She enters during the Elm season with its over-riding qualities of fertility, purification, protection, and right action. Little wonder she creates the urge to begin anew! Her powers of protection were honoured in New Year fires that drove away evil spirits, and birch fires too were used to beat the bounds round villages in Spring. The birch was associated with Spring in general. On Imbolc at the start of February, the womenfolk placed a "Bride" or corn dolly together with a wand of birch in a basket. Then they would call "Let Bride come in! Bride is Welcome!". In the morning, they would rake the ashes of the fire for signs of footprints. If none were found, they gave offerings at the hearth to appease her spirit.

Robert Graves suggested that the Ogham calendar is based on the Beth-Luis-Nion alphabet, and that Beth, or Birch, is the first letter. Life begins with Birch, drawing upon the great healing present in the womb of the Earth. Let us journey towards new life asking for Gaia's blessings, as we create an embryo of the new Human that will burst forth in the Ash month that follows later in the spring. This is the time for making plans for the future, for making new projects. It asks us to search for our highest intentions.

Rowan LUIS

Now we enter the waxing half of the year, and darkness is in rapid recess. The rowan summons bright sunrays into the year, encouraging growth again. The rowan represents the incarnating individual. She works with intermediary powers in assisting a soul's passage from one world to the next. Thus her name "the quickening tree". The rowan is ruled by the Sun and is seen as a protector. She protects us against malevolent forces through operating a magic of the highest and purest calibre. With an incarnating soul this was of utmost importance.

Her magic protects against enchantment in many situations. For instance, often you can find a rowan growing near stone circles. She protects ley lines that often run through stone circles. She acts as a go-between the elemental and human worlds. The rowan is able to look into both worlds simultaneously. The rowan calls upon the powers that dwell in the devic world to work with her so she can help us all.

Her ability helps us in the threshold situations we face in birth and death. She helps humans give birth in the final stages, when a process of quickening takes place. Conversely, during the death process she can prolong life and protect you against death. During this time of year we are chiefly concerned with new life and the incarnating individual.

Dwelling in the element of Fire, her long life invigorates and blesses all she touches. Qualities of healing, protecting and controlling of the senses all aid her mission. Her strong sense of will helps us fully birth new projects, grounding and protecting us and bringing success in its wake.

Above all, this feisty new woman is here to help humanity gain purpose and direction. Her cohort, the ash, will follow.

The rowan is similar to the apple tree on both a physical (botanical family is the Pomoideae group) and metaphysical (mythical) level. The apple is more or less opposite the rowan on the calendar. Often we find trees with similar properties facing each other across the calendar year.

The rowan illustrates its ability to protect in a tale of Diarmid and Grainne: They entered a magical forest and met Sharvan a giant, who forbade them to eat the rowan berries growing there. Diarmid managed to kill the giant and collect berries for Grainne. They then once again escaped Grainne's husband Fionn who was chasing them, and they went safely on their way.

Ash NION

The ash supports the birth of animals. Still in the Elm season, and still ruled by the Sun, the ash actively links the inner and outer worlds. The Warrior succeeds due to a hidden female aspect supporting him. He is being prepared for his role in the world, with the brave women behind him! This androgynous tree copes with the adversity of life – a physical example would be how she can find water with her long roots. Her fire has the quality of the goddess, and illuminating powers, for she favours the light. When setting out on any endeavour, reaching for the light is paramount. In Norse mythology Ygdrassil is an ash tree at the centre of their world. She connects nine levels of existence, heavily guarded by serpents.

In Irish mythology there were five magical trees planted by Fintan. One in the North is an oak, one in the South is a yew, and three in the centre are ash. These represent the three levels or kingdoms to which we belong. I suspect that those three levels can be subdivided into three more levels each. Then we have the nine as in Norse mythology.

However the ash is dying back, as is the elm, its seasonal tree, which succumbed to Dutch Elm disease some decades before. It is interesting that both these trees belong to the beginning of the solar year, and are vulnerable now to disease. I feel it is symbolic of a new large cycle that has not yet begun and so the trees that commence the cycle have lost their confidence to survive. This also hints at the ongoing natural chaos of our planet. When we don't work with nature, nature will respond with messages. We need to heal the severance with our natural world. We need to rekindle the hidden lunar qualities of the ash that have been superseded by masculine worldly powers. When the ash is in balance, humanity will have its true leaders. We know the ancestors were familiar with the deeper primeval levels of existence. Our success in endeavours now necessitates a process of rebirth and regeneration.

The ash is also ruled by the element of water, with its strong lunar associations. Her oldest memories are primeval and lunar. She can help translate the past and realign our present realities into a wise future. If we are to remain in tune with a wider cosmos, the ash is the tree to reunite us with our higher destiny. She also can help us accept the power of our dreams, and can help us work with the stresses in our lives. In short, she has a leading role in bringing humanity to the Fountain of Life. For the following season of Summer to flow, we invoke the spirit of the ash now.

Alder FEARN

The alder is entering the Gorse season, which firmly belongs to the Warrior spirit. Ruled by Venus, the warrior is protecting everyone else. This tree gravitates toward darkness and so links with the underworld and death. This is not a natural death as at the end of a life cycle, but a premature death borne either of sacrifice or initiation. Pythagorus underwent initiatory rites when he visited Orpheus. According to Robert Graves, this occurred under an alder.

Bran the Alder led those fighting on the side of darkness in the epic poem Battle of the Trees (early Welsh). Bran is patron saint of bards who shielded the rest of the tribe from truth too harsh to face. This reminds us of our subconscious that we cannot assimilate into full consciousness. The alder acts as a guardian between worlds. He grows by water, yet is not of the water, for he is water-resilient. He burns with a smouldering fire and an undercurrent heat. This energy sustains one through the trials and tribulations of life.

The previous ash in her female aspects can veer into states of lunacy if unchecked. Now the alder that follows her is a shield against lunacy, and many other things. In fact, the Gaelic for alder is "fearn", also meaning a shield.

The alder shares the ash's affinity with water. In many ways, the alder and ash resemble the qualities of a king and queen respectively. Yet the alder is an unassuming tree that clings to the shade, and his true power is overlooked. As Bran the Alder in myth ruled the mysterious underworld, it is revealing to examine his speeches. They seem to belong to an older consciousness. Aligning with Brigit, Bran was patron saint of bards, whose speeches were of the old, clairvoyant kind that shielded the rest of humanity from truths too deep to accept in normal everyday life.

So how willing are we to embrace the underworld? How willing are we to look into our own subconscious? Consider how the alder lives near water, and at the same time is remarkably resilient to water. In the same way the alder shields us from knowing too much about our subconscious, allowing us instead to grow under its influence in a healthy manner. It is this firm quality that shields us from the lunacy of seeing too much!

Willow SAILLE (twinned with Blackthorn STRAIF)

Continuing with the Gorse season, we now are fully in the flow of life. The willow assists with flow of life by remaining positive amidst change. She exhibits many positive attributes. She supports the building of community over and above the individual. Her work is much needed now. In true peace-maker style, she facilitates neutrality and forgives injustice. She reconciles opposites and creates harmony and balance. Rods of justice in Druidic times were named "wicker" rods, since they were crafted from willow. The word "wicca" stems from her name.

The willow carries an aspect of death in life, which many would associate with the unknown aspect of life, with the subconscious. And it also carries an aspect of life in death, which carries much wisdom and insight. Like her predecessor the alder, she welcomes darkness. Her aspirin deadens the pain. The Moon rules her, and she is associated with night visions, psychic powers and fecundity. She is the first tree that bees visit for pollen; one ought to take note, since bees are such sacred creatures.

Blackthorn STRAIF (twinned with Willow SAILLE)

Note that this bears a double S aspect of willow. In effect, the Willow has shifted from the aspect of the Fecund Woman to a more masculine, potent version of Woman, often seen as the Old Hag. The blackthorn amplifies the aspects of the willow, and takes it to a new level, combining the strength of her gentle qualities and his own firmer male qualities. Her fecundity transmutes into the Will aspect of the female, as personified in the re-emergence of the Old Hag. She offers detachment, ruled by Saturn and the diametrically opposed Mars. Her fruit, a Mars-like Sloe (as used in sloe gin), is considered less benevolent than aspirin of the willow!

It's interesting that the blackthorn shares the same Ogham as the elder at the end of the year. Both are connected with rebirth. Here the battles fought in youth have ended, and the soul prepares for the next stage of its incarnation. There is fresh purpose in the female guardian's stride, aided by power, shape-shifting and discernment. She purges negativity, leaving one pure.

Following the willow that gently dissipated pain, quietly encouraging growth and healing, now we shift to the more challenging inner work that will rid us of our symptoms. This necessary inner work purges us deeper by tackling the root causes of our imbalance: negative thoughts. As a blackthorn, we meet pain with dignity. We embrace the quality of the season and amplify it, cleansing ourselves of issues holding us back. Often this cleansing can feel severe as we clear deep energy blockages through sheer determination.

In these times there is no place for negativity. We need to cultivate the inner strength to overcome our outworn patterns. Since the Gorse season is upon us, the battle continues on the interior. We strive here for success. We cannot move on, so we stay ever so still in our molten inner state, and trust. This then is the real test, when we meet ourselves in our hour of need, and call upon inner resources that only rarely surface. They are there.

Hawthorn HUATH

The hawthorn introduces the Heather season, which is ruled by Venus. She herself is ruled by Mars. Her cohort is Bel the Sun god celebrated at Beltaine. The theme of warriors continues with this female warrior tree. Like the blackthorn before her, the hawthorn is a great discerner. She transforms the smouldering fire of the blackthorn into a raging fire that burns fiercer than any other tree. The fecundity of the hawthorn lived in the depths of our imagination during the time of the blackthorn. Now it moves into the realm of the physical and becomes raw sexual power, coupled with the complex power of female intuition. Orchestrating a crescendo of Spring in her wake, the Hawthorn brings us daydreams, spurs our faerie feet to wander, and promises sacred union. Her profuse blossoms remind us of her generous spirit, over-shadowing the delicate white flowers her sister tree, the blackthorn, yielded earlier.

The hawthorn's magic grants happiness, somehow linked to the Otherworld. Concerned with the community at large, her own destiny is bound up with human destiny. Land-owners ascribed powers of protection to the tree. The hawthorn has beggared protection through the ages. Historically, hereditary rights were bound up in the tree. If a bard was ill-treated by their king they held council on a hill overlooking the lands. A hawthorn grew at the centre and each bard held a slingshot and thorn. If the ground swallowed them up they were wrong; if not the king forfeited his titles!

In Ireland farmers still are respectful of her elemental powers, fearing the wrath of the fairies if they cut her down.

The complex spirit of the hawthorn is not led astray by external events that fluctuate. There is a rich tapestry of energies that underlie the natural order, and nature's cohort, the hawthorn, creates order from the depths of nature's chaos. She does not do this through logic or direct intent. Her inspiration comes from a love spun on Spring breezes of hope and potential. She creates beauty and order in our world through positivity, love, compassionate warmth, and sweet tenderness. All of this is bound up with her highly developed intuition. It is such a scene of gaiety and bohemian joy. Her pulse of natural order can cure human heart disorders. It is all about restoring the weary and dreaming new realities into existence.

Oak DUIR

Following the hawthorn who laid the foundations for order, the Oak restores structure. This is thanks to Saturn his ruler. Fittingly, the great early diplomat St. Columba came from the Place of the Oak (Derry). There is something intensely grounding and gratifying about the oak. Our fractured world needs him. It is the most commonly chosen archetype for a tree, for it represents physical and mental vigour in life, stability, protection and generosity of spirit. Moreover it embraces communality, structure and form. His natural ease, stability, courage and confidence appeals to most souls.

His ruling element is the Earth, shared by the last tree in the cycle the elder, and also by the Elm Season at the start of the year. Positioned at the midpoint of the year, the oak represents the incarnation of ideas. He is diametrically opposed to the birch at the start of the year who represents the incarnation of the individual. The oak incarnates the astral rather than physical realms.

The air-borne mistletoe likes to grow on oak, hawthorn, apple and yew. The oak is linked with Dagda the god of thunder, while mistletoe is associated with its accompanying lightning strikes. When the Druids conferred in their groves, it is believed that the only god they invited to enter was Dagda, the god of thunder. The green man is an element of Dagda. He is the thunder god of Gaia, attracted to the oak, that most noble tree. Even if he struck the oak, it could re-leaf itself. The oak and mistletoe are indeed complementary to one another.

According to mystic Rudolf Steiner, the mistletoe is the Christ essence that also resides in each of us. It protects us, facilitates our deeper meditations and helps us overcome adversity as we reach into our new states of being IN LOVE. It was the early Celts who, when trading for Baltic amber, first encountered a cult centred around the oak. Later their coffins carried ceremonial sprigs of oak and mistletoe.

The oak carries the collective efforts and qualities of the previous trees to fruition in an act of almost effortless courage. Sometimes we let our inner strength slip away, often when we lose our connection to our higher reality. When that happens, we forget that all is perfect, and we lose our confidence, our trust, and our sense of being comfortable and connected.

Especially in these times when our realities are splintering and our boats are being rocked, we can regain control of our lives in a way that is nurturing our growth by calling on the energies of the oak. The oak tree carries the vibration that all is well. It protects us, and guides us through our manmade nightmares. If we seek direction and purpose in our lives, we can look to the oak for an ally.

The future kingdom is upon us now. The holly is waiting in the wings with his Mars-like energy, ready to usurp the oak, and create a new kingdom of his own for the second half of the year. Yet it is wise not to overlook the oak, with its detached loving-kindness, and all the other trees working together to bring about an evolution in consciousness.

The oak played a pivotal role in ancient European cultures. Now a new race is in a perpetual state of creation, as the goddess Dione returns more and more to her full power. Her double aspect as the receiver and the giver recreates, then supports, a new oak. The alchemical process takes place at midsummer, when the gap between the oak and holly is filled with a higher heart and an acute spiritual potency. It is the quality rather than the quantity of acorns that will measure human progress. The female goddess lends her support to the oak in its whole aspect of being, allowing its potential to blossom, while Dagda the god of thunder lends his skills to connect with and ignite the oak in the first place.

Holly TINNE

After the oak, that gentle giant of the tree archetypes, comes the fiery wee holly. The holly is a tree less noticeable than the oak in a forest. Yet he is a true fighter, offering the strongest protection. Ruled by benevolent Mars and the fire element, he can be compared to the green knight Gawain in Arthurian tales. I see the holly representing inner fire. In Christianity, he is the Christ that his predecessor John the Baptist (the oak) prepared the way for. It has to be remembered that Christ was a secretive and elusive force in society in his day. Similarly, the holly king prepared the oak king Cuchulain for his rule in Celtic mythology.

The holly like the oak is a benevolent guardian. The two trees are like father and son, the holly being the offspring of the oak. The holly has a distinguishing feature: an element of surprise. In the wider scheme of things you could say that humanity is entering a holly cycle now. The holly energy can constantly wreck our mundane lives and habits. By highlighting any residual anger and defensiveness in us, the holly sets about transforming these feelings into a victorious love. This is a truly alchemical process.

This love is the purest, what I call the Christic essence. It is what frees us from the endless round of human emotions that hold us back from reaching our full potential. Now that the second half of the year is beginning, the earth will support us more in our endeavours to go inward and grow toward spirit. We become less earth-bound and more heaven-bound, until we reach the point when the holly shines its berries for us at Christmas/the Winter Solstice.

The oak king is twinned with the Holly prince who is poised to threaten the oak's supremacy at Midsummer. Then there is an extra day inserted into the year, over which no tree presides. This is the day when the elementals rule the Earth. If the Holly prince wins, a completely new set of twelve trees will take over the cycle. However, so far the thirteen trees remain, as mankind has not made the shift to a more stable paradigm yet. The oak and the holly hover either side of Midsummer's Day, a day that transports the Otherworld into our own dimension. The holly is borne from the gap that Midsummer's Day serves, and so the holly is seen as a wild man born between worlds. In the human world, Christians associated John the Baptist with the first or waxing half of the year and Christ with the waning half. John the Baptist was a necessary component who established an interface between Heaven and Earth, whereas the Christ embodied Heaven on Earth.

In an oak wood in summer the holly lies beneath the leaf canopy, hidden and secretive. Although we now are in summer, it is in winter that the holly comes into its own when its berries light up the wintry landscape. It is as if it reaches into the earth itself to bring forth its cosmic signature. The celestial core of the earth blesses the holly as protector divine, as our wise guide. It guards the precious energy of life itself but we don't recognize it if we harbour wounding thoughts against others or ourselves. The holly is calling us to reconnect with our higher selves, now more than ever! We need to still our inner beings and reach the point at which the holly starts its regal procession.

Listen to the holly, for the mysteries of regeneration and rebirth are stored within it. Imagine the holly growing in a secret grove, and place yourself alongside it, in harmony with its stillness and deep wisdom.

Hazel COLL (twinned with Apple QUERT)

After the benign warrior-like qualities of the oak and holly, we start to progress toward the end of the year where the more inward qualities start to reveal themselves more. The hazel is a deeply sacred tree. This noble tree is ruled by the Sun and by the Air element. Her gift is to find what is hidden. More predominant in the west of Ireland, the hazel continues bringing forth the inner qualities. The locations of trees within the calendar also hint at their qualities. The west is more concerned with the Yin aspects of life, so qualities such as wisdom and reflection come to the fore. The east is more yang, so qualities such as courage and impulsiveness are more dominant.

The number nine is deeply associated with the hazel tree. Her lunar month falls within the ninth solar month. Nine is the number for completion, or utmost wisdom. In Celtic myth, nine spots appeared on the salmon's body where hazelnuts fell upon her. The hazel offers us intuition; her nuts, ruled by Mercury, represent knowledge and wisdom. Divination is one of her key properties; in Halloween the nuts were used to divine the future.

The hazel has the power to bring forth the psychic qualities of the Earth, and then communicate these to us. The relative innocuous appearance of the hazel is deceptive, for it stores wisdom and inspiration that feeds our poetry and music. It is her concealing of the deeper truth that is key to understanding how the hazel augments the qualities of the holly that preceded it. Its innate ability to find what is hidden means that it can work with intuition to reach that elusive individuality the holly introduced. The Celtic trees encourage us on our path. Each one exposes us to certain qualities, and any non-resolved issues are carried forward where our next tree archetype offers us further opportunities to work on them.

As we go into the second half of the year, the inner qualities become more important. During the hazel time, some homage is paid to dreams. We are almost upon the Aspen season or Autumn season, when the unknown rises to our attention.

Apple QUERT (twinned with Hazel COLL)

Ruled by Venus, the apple is concerned with healing, love, self-love and self-acceptance. These qualities are often found when alone at the end of life's journey. The wild apple too often grows alone in the wilderness. The apple tree is the wild twin sister of the hazel. As a double consonant ruled by the Water element, the wild apple tree magnifies and shares the magic spun by the hazel in the twilight zone. Now let's dwell a while in the twilight zone with the earth wisdom and magic of these dual trees.

The apple stands opposite the enchanting rowan in the calendar. Like the rowan, the apple tends to grow near stone circles. It is associated with Avalon and Eternal Life. The polarity between the apple and the rowan is one that deepens destiny.

Mistletoe/Vine MUIN

Mistletoe follows the hazel/apple duo. It is an epiphyte and does not feed from soil, but rather gains nutrients from the air. This is so apt, as the apple is the most common tree host for the mistletoe, and is herself regarded as the goddess of the orchard.

Having felt the call of cosmic love and divine connection in the apple, we reach the mistletoe so clearly sprung from the world of spirit. As might be expected, this plant is ruled by the Air element under the guidance of the Sun. It aligns you with your higher vibrations so you can reach a visionary state of mind. Like Christ in action, it is perfection in humility, rootless yet driven by the purest state of love we can experience.

A great healer, mistletoe is used in treatment of both cancer and Aids. Regarded as a charm against evil, it has been found placed in burial mounds as a ritual object. It sits comfortably in the Aspen season, with its emphasis on matters of death and the shadow.

It can serve to align us with our higher purpose.

Ivy GORT

We are now in the season of the Aspen, and the aspects of Air and Mercury dominate the ivy. Ivy represents the eternal feminine principle in action. The ivy is very strong and wily. It is the last plant to embrace the shadow in a purposeful way. All aspects of life and death, shadow and light, come together here. She often is in holy partnership with the holly, who beckons us to a spiritual birth. She forms a right angle with the holly in the Calendar. This angle hints at a shift we can make now to resurrect those aspects of ourselves not yet redeemed.

This intensely feminine plant lies in the west of our chart directly opposite the Green Man, the alder, in the East. The ivy is our wise woman, our green goddess, whose roots are earthbound. She spirals endlessly. It reminds me of the eternal searching of the soul for enlightenment. Success comes to the degree that the other tree lessons have been assimilated. The Hag displays a wily wit that helps us overcome all odds we may face in life.

We have reached the stage of life when there will be states of frenzy as we encounter other realms and states of being that are unfamiliar and unbound to earth. There is method in the madness. The timely periods of intoxication serve to loosen ties to this world, in order to move round the life cycle. The Halloween witches spring to mind as the symbol for the energy encountered here. The Yew season of death enters here.

Broom/Reed NGETAL

Now we prepare to walk past the receding light of Samhain. Moon and Water predominate. Little is known about the two plants that are said to represent this lunar month. The two contenders for its title are both obscure. The broom was considered excellent for boosting the immune system, and was known as Physician's Strength! The changing of the seasons from mild to cooler often brings disease with it. During Spring, the delicate and fragrant blooms of the broom are prolific, as if nature is bestowing a blessing on the world. Could it be that our ancients perceived a potent, non-physical gift in the broom plant at this time of year? We can embody characteristics of decay with a waning Sun, so she is welcome. She has a male counterpart in the reed.

The reed is the second possible plant to represent this month. It probably was more commonly associated with this month. Nevertheless, its meaning is quite mysterious; the reed requires our imagination to understand him more. Its long, straight appearance reminds me of a singular executive strike of a hammer, or a spear flying through the air. Such action is necessary for a plan to unfold. In this case, the strike announces the flight our soul takes on the final part of our earthly journey. After the intense and ultimately transformative struggles the ivy stoically bears, the reed offers us sovereignty at last.

The reed is also seen as the archivist because manuscripts were written with reeds. It would fit that the reed keeps a record of one's life at this stage of the cycle.

Elder RUIS

Following on from the more male analytical lunar month of the reed Scribe, we now swing over to another female lunar month, that of the elder. Appropriately named, this is the thirteenth and final tree month in our Ogham calendar. This thirteenth tree is strongly associated with death and regeneration. The spiritual meaning of death is nowadays neglected in society. With no doubt the old hag is transforming into the young maiden yet again, guided by Venus. She is embedded in the hidden Underworld of the Earth while across the cycle, the oak is associated with the Overworld. The Earth element rules both trees.

The elder is perhaps the most intriguing tree to behold and explore. Associated somewhat negatively with witchcraft and death in recent times, the elder is in fact a deeply thoughtful and philosophical tree, of great integrity and honesty.

There are strong fairy associations here. Whilst the elder does not burn with a strong physical heat, its fire is strong in another dimension that is not of the human realm. This fairy fire stokes the flames of inner courage and acceptance. Above all other trees it claims its shadow without guilt, and offers an extraordinary mix of extravert wild abandon and a deep inward seeking that forces her to withdraw from the physical senses, despite offering many practical uses and remedies.

Despite the ignorant connotations with bad luck, number 13 in mysticism marks an essential shift of consciousness, providing a transitory state that then transforms an original stable 12 into a new stable set of 12. This knowledge is beyond the remit of this book, but I have alluded to it when discussing the oak and also will return to the theme in the final chapter.

Chapter 5

The Energetics of Sound

Why use sound? "Healing" sounds bypass the brain and work with the "heart mind". This term describes a state of being created when right-brain and left-brain activity merge. In fact, listening to sound can be a form of mindfulness, for it can still the mind. Sound can activate your more intuitive side, since the mind is not dominating. Moreover, sound healing can expand the energy field of an environment or person in an instant! This enhances the experience of being present and aware.

It follows that sound healing is an effective vehicle for communing with the trees. First let us consider what sound does in the etheric, or energy, field.

The Sound Ether

"In the beginning was the Word, and the Word was with God and the Word was God."

The beginning of St. John's gospel has always resonated with me. I intuit that St. John was referring to a set of divine vibrations that created every living thing. When he wrote about "the word", he was writing about vibrations rather than specific words. If we view the word as a vocal sound that echoed the original sound, we are perhaps nearing the truth of its meaning. I can imagine the divine creator initiated sounds, which set up vibratory fields. These energy fields created all matter in their wake. It follows that sound therapy may be an effective vehicle for communing with all matter, including the trees.

According to spiritual law, form follows thought. So, an original thought must have created each tree within the Celtic Tree Calendar. Here I am considering the process of creation in which trees came into being on Earth. Sound is a denser vibration than inaudible vibration. As far as I understand it, sound mediates between form and thought. A divine thought carries its own etheric vibration. By concentrating a thought pattern, the vibration could intensify into a sound. This further densified and brought the natural tree form into being.

Everything vibrates at some frequency, including trees and plants. In the distant past there were no technological distractions. Could it be that our ancestors perceived sounds and vibrations far more acutely than we do? Could they hear a sound range that only the bird and animal kingdom hear now? Even in present times people have auditory experiences around trees. It is more likely to occur when you are at peace with the natural environment in which you encounter the trees. When you approach the plant kingdom with reverence, a space opens up for the unexpected to occur. I recall entering a local grove of beech trees with a guest who was keen to play some gongs with me by the river. As we walked in, a tree in the distance started to emit a flapping sound that was not due to any force of nature. It sounded like sheets of thin metal shaken in a rhythmic manner. It was a paranormal sound that we both experienced but did not share until later. Dowsing the area revealed energetic anomalies. Instances in which trees "speak" are rare for me. I tend to create sounds for the trees and then dowse for their auric response. I am clair-olfactory though, and trees have emitted wonderful etheric aromas on occasions!

I am fascinated at how trees became so sacred to the Druids. There must have been some real spiritual experiences to go with this core belief. Did the Druids perceive tree vibrations as part of their training? Perhaps they even devised meditation techniques to identify "core sounds" or vibrations. How did they perceive these vibrations to emanate from a divine source? I can imagine the elders spending a lot of their waking time in the forest, dwelling in the silence. They would relish this silence as they tapped into subtle "core sounds" with their inner ear. I use tuning forks in a similar fashion to determine such core sounds.

Before I discuss tuning forks, I want to consider the Celtic Tree alphabet. How were letters arrived at? I see it as a sculpturing of sounds. Vowel sounds emerge from the human body without any modification of our vocal chords. Hence the vowels are a purer sound than any of the consonants. Vowel sounds are closer to the essence of our being. In many religions people based the name for God on pure vowel sounds. Robert Graves, that great classicist and poet, scrutinized the Celtic tree vowels. He deduced that the early Celts called God "Jehovah". Graves included two double vowels (AA and II) to pronounce the name phonetically. This is the Latinization of the Hebrew word for God: Yahweh!

When plotting the tree letters within a yearly cycle, a pattern emerges as shown in the Diagram on page 10. Each month is named after a particular tree. The various qualities ascribed to each tree are revealing. They lead from one tree to the next, revealing a meaningful pattern. The qualities flow into one another and present a whole picture of a composite being. It is as if seeing behind creation, into a world of thought forms. The trees representing the thoughts formed themselves into a world of beauty.

Robert Graves suggests that the Druids created their early alphabet based on runes, comprised of thirteen consonants and five vowels, more or less. There were some double consonants. The name for each tree in his Celtic Tree calendar began with a different vowel or consonant. It was these initial letters that form the basis of the OGHAM (pronounced "AUM") alphabet that he proposed. In Hinduism, Aum is the sound of the cosmic creator. "Aum" is the synthesis of all the sounds of highly vibrating life forces. Moreover, many have perceived Aum to be the Word in the opening of the Gospel of St. John.

The purpose of most extant runes in the UK and Ireland is to record the genealogy of a person. Inscribed on a stone they mark his final resting place. It is easy to overlook the fact that there must have been a process of determining the sound for the rune in the first place. It is this aspect that fascinates me. During that period, some in the culture were interested in the cosmic dimensions of the Earth. Perhaps the early Druids could hear divine vibrations in matter. When I compare my own experience at sacred sites, it offers a parallel to refer to. I have discovered core energies at ancient sacred sites. These fine energies have been over-layered at times with other denser energies. Human thought patterns would have created such denser vibrations. Whenever people lose their connection to source, the thoughts generated are denser. This happens when people think without being in a state of pure or prayerful intent. Their mundane thoughts amplify during powerful rituals, and deposit a denser layer of energy. The residual lower density energy creates a sub layer of energy at a site, which people can tune into. Some people feel called to clear such sites through a healing ritual. But it is actually possible to bypass the dross and tune into the core-energy. This layer is beautiful, untainted by false, ungodly, or unnatural thinking. I discovered many years ago I had a natural capacity to align with the core energy of a place. The core energy of sacred sites is universal and strong, and perceptible to many people. Often there is an air of sanctity in a site that emanates from the divine source, though not everyone can sense it. People who do sense its rare vibration are capable of resonating with the core energy. The core energy is pure and bears a divine, eternal quality.

Similarly, quiet places in nature and even single trees emit a core sound. The core sound stems from the timeless realm. This might be subtler to tap into than at a potent site, but nonetheless it is there. I propose the Druids ascribed core sounds to each of the various tree species. Hence an alphabet of core sounds arose. First the Druids might have vocalized the sounds they heard with their internal ears. Those sounds over time would have become common knowledge. Not only were the Druids attuned to nature; they also lived closer to the subconscious realms. The elementals live in the realm of the subconscious and of nature. They could have influenced the naming of the trees.

If we go much further back in time, the original races on Earth may have named their trees too. At what point did their names become a cultural response to their perceptions of the trees? Surely originally the tree actually emitted a sound that early Man perceived? As time progressed I imagine that each new race named trees according to how they resonated. For instance, as a young woman working in Japan I sensed their language contains a deep sense of awe for nature. It has an unsophisticated, almost child-like word structure, consisting of alternating vowels and consonants.

It seems an early language when man's consciousness was entwined with nature. If we look at a modern language such as French, the name for "tree" is "arbre". This gives a sense of wonder and heart expansion when you say it. When we say the English word "tree" we start with a hard "t', which is very grounding, followed by an intense "ee" sound. This connects more to the throat chakra. If you compare the two cultures you can see how their words for the same object, the tree, differ. The different resonances of each culture manifests in the language. So the Ogham sounds might give us some insights into the Druid culture if we take enough time to study it. I recommend the research of vibrational healer Fabian Maman. Fabian has studied the energetic imprints behind names, and his research is fascinating.

When we are in an elevated state of awareness we can perceive the initial or core sounds of trees. I realize that this may well be daunting as a goal. We should create the space to listen well for the vibrations, or sounds, that emanate in nature. Do not doubt your imagination when you are in a deep listening state. Noise surrounds us often, and yet it is worth our while to return to simple nature.

We can approach a place with an open heart and mind to hear its essential core energy as a vibratory sound. Our minds can then translate it into a note closest to mirroring that frequency.

Reconnecting to Nature through Sound

When I tune into a tree, I use a set of chromatic steel tuning forks. I strike each one of the forks in turn against the trunk of a tree. I am listening for clarity, purity of tone, and strength in the quality of the sound. I listen for this in a similar way with an individual when I am in a sound healing session. By a process of elimination I am able to select the fork(s) that resonate best with the tree. This is what I call the essential sound, or essence of the tree. It is how I imagine the Druids might have named their trees in ancient times. They chose a sound that reflected the essence of the tree. In my case I am selecting a pure tone to reflect the essence. I know from dowsing sacred sites that to detect the core vibration you have to become like an empty vessel, adopting a neutral stance. Try not to let any thoughts or feelings distract you, as this can colour your perceptions.

I have found some ways of exploring the individual energies of the trees. Once I led a group walk where we noticed a tree that had lost a branch, either due to vandalism or natural storm damage. I use a set of chromatic tuning forks, such as a piano tuner would use. Striking each fork in turn against the tree, I felt through my heart which forks matched the vibration of the tree. I selected two forks that were only a semitone apart. I had not realized this until I had gone through the selection process. (I know from my work as a sound healer that playing two forks together on the human body can break up pain. In such a case, the musical interval is only a dissonant semitone.) The group then toned the notes of both forks together to create the dissonance. The tree clearly had needed this sound because it was in pain. We dowsed the energy field around the tree before and after our toning. We found the aura had greatly expanded. I next exchanged the second original fork with a new fork. The new fork duo was a harmonic interval apart, and then we toned this combination to the tree. The aura expanded even further. This method of using forks to direct your tones achieves healing and balancing for the trees. It also is a great way of becoming more present with the tree. Generally with this method it is best not to work it out with your head. Instead strike each fork in the chromatic scale one by one, sensing how the sound speaks in your heart. It is after all through the fundamental energy of love that we often receive higher knowledge.

Intention is paramount in all healing work, whether alone or in groups. At times it is hard to achieve perfect synergy in toning. People may not be able to hold a note if someone else is singing a secondary note. In that case I try not to be too critical, as that would defeat the object. In the early days of this work, I was too focused on the quality of the sound we were creating. I am sure the outcome suffered on such occasions! After delivering more tree workshops, I learnt that intent is key. I started to lose my deadly grip on details and techniques!

A heart-felt connection is paramount to understanding how energy works. You can of course dowse the tree with your voice, without using the forks at all. Approach the tree while focusing on your heart centre. Then open your mouth to allow any sound to issue forth. Imagine that you are singing from your heart centre to the heart of the tree. Often one tone in particular will create a deeper resonance with the tree. Continue with that one tone for as long as you feel is right.

This form of toning is also possible in a group situation. Again, intent is key. However, when people tone in a group it can be quite messy at the start. It is a challenge to become that collective empty vessel or conduit for any prolonged period. It is perhaps wise to introduce vocal toning after the group has gelled. People need to feel comfortable with toning from their hearts. It is not a performance but a service to nature. Aim at becoming a synergy heart vessel, allowing the sound to pass through with ease. Sound is best used sparingly for a greater effect. It is the quality of heart-centred sound, not the quantity or volume of sound we make that counts.

It would be interesting to approach the same tree with two different groups. The first group could perform the toning exercise using forks. The second group could ignore the forks and meditate in silence near the tree at first. In this way they can reach a deep level of resonance with the tree before toning. If the tones chosen by the two groups matched, it would show how easy it is to tap into the trees, using the universal language of sound. Such experiments would encourage us to use sound in our exploration of the natural world. I personally find using the forks helps focus me in the short window of time I have during a workshop scenario.

Some years ago I trained in various modules of sonic acupuncture with Fabian Maman. This master sound healer invented the term "vibrational healing" in the 1980s. When I told him I suspected that there were core tones present in natural objects, he concurred. I had discovered core tones for trees, wells and other sacred sites in general. He told me that he introduces a similar method to his students at the end of their long official training. I seem to have a soul affinity with the work. It may explain why when I was younger I had vivid dreams of toning a dying landscape back into life. At that time the notion of sound healing was non-existent where I lived!

Trees or plants, whether big or small, carry their own music or language. Observe a tree or plant. If you can let yourself go, and listen in a relaxed but intent manner, you may imagine you hear a feint noise. Try to emulate this noise, and the tree will enjoy your mirroring of its inner music. I have tried this and a person beside me felt currents of energy shoot up her spine as I did so. When we attune to the vibrations of a plant or tree we are working with our elemental self. This forms part of our own energy field. Our elemental self is naturally aligned with the forces that sustain life in the plant world. Tree language is like nothing we can equate to our human world. It is like a string of incomprehensible syllables that vary in tone, and are not sustained notes. It is an etheric language, both earthly and other-worldly. Everything contained within the cosmos is also found within the Earth. When trees lay their deep roots they pick up these cosmic forces more than other plants.

I am convinced that trees thrive on our warm attention. They enjoy our acknowledging and appreciating them. Gaia includes the feelings and thoughts of plants, humans, animals and so much more. Since everything connects with one another, communication is possible. Our imagination will find a way of communicating.

Unfortunately, schools sometimes emphasize a mechanistic view of science that looks at laws of cause and effect, and stresses the importance of categorizing everything. However this approach can ignore our interconnectivity. Nevertheless we are part of nature and vice versa. If we do not engage with the reality of this complexity, we ignore it at our peril.

Advanced research in physics continually reveals how consciousness pervades all living things. Marko Pogacnik, who I know as a friend, has researched this subject for most of his adult life. He addresses a latent human need to enter into dialogue with nature. In the next section I describe how I have adapted his work to help you make a deep connection with the trees.

Gongs are marvellous instruments because they contain so many tones within them. I was fortunate to buy a gong that my teacher had selected in China. It contains very rich tones. When a gong holds many overtones it ensures that the right tones will reach where they need to go. Further, each of the planets in our solar system emits radio wave lengths of very low frequencies that can be detected with special equipment. My gong is tuned in with the natural harmonic series of the planet Pluto. In other words, it is resonant with the planetary vibrations emitted by Pluto. Pluto bears the qualities of purification, letting go and integration, all necessary for transformation. This made perfect sense to me as I have always been drawn to inner work for transformation.

I have taken the gong several times to play by the river that runs below a beech woodland. On a subtle level water can gather the sounds and store them for posterity. Soon after that point on the river, the entire body of water cascades underneath the hillside! The river runs through rare limestone features and its journey ends down a swallow hole. So playing the gong just before the point at which the river dives underground feels like sending a gift to Gaia. I have a complementary gong that is more yang in nature. One day a colleague and I were playing the gongs beside the river. The mature beech trees grew on the steep banks above us. When we ceased, a deep thudding beat continued to resound at least ten minutes. The beat resounded in our hearts too. It was like we were embodying the quality of the landscape through our heart resonance. It was a blessed experience.

Trees are the chiefs of the plant tribe, and they can heal humans. Trees equally can appreciate humans sending them rich tones of a gong. After playing the gong to a tree, the aura usually expands a lot. If you encounter a tree growing alone, you may feel it to be un-nurtured. You can boost its resonance by playing a drum made of animal skin. I play a buffalo skin drum around a large collapsed river cave, where the trees growing on the edge of the deep rim are relatively isolated. They are not able to grow in a normal forest community. I intuitively played the drum at first. Later I learnt that playing a drum cultivates feminine, nurturing aspects. This seems to be an appropriate way to help heal lonely trees.

The Role of Intention

Sound, especially music, is a wonderful life-enhancing medium. Many would feel bereft without sound. We all know sound consists of vibrations. We overlook the fact that our collective and individual intention also transmits vibrations. Thought is energy, and will imprint a vibratory code in the ether. For instance, when we "speak" to plants we are sending out thoughts that can help them thrive. The plants can feel our thoughts vibrating toward them, and they respond well to loving intent. In my experience our intention adds power to our communications. It is no different when communing with our biggest plants: the trees. I would go as far to say that *intention* is the key ingredient in our communication with nature. Whether playing gongs, drums, or using voice in nature, the player's intention is paramount. It would be interesting to compare different ways of using sound when communing with plants. We could try using sound alone, intention alone, or combining sound with intention. Again, I would use dowsing as my preferred tool to check the effect on their auric fields.

There seems to be a growing desire for people to draw closer to nature in ways that are perceptible to the senses. Surely at this stage scientists need to pay more attention to our less visible worlds. They could set out to prove the existence of subtle energies, and measure the power of intention. There are many subtle forces of energy that exist in our multi-layered nature arena. Nature has an intelligence that is aware of our intentions, until proven otherwise.

Chapter 6

GAIA TOUCH WITH TREES

For most of my life I have felt there had to be a way of connecting our own light bodies with those of the Earth's. We were not separate from the living earth, and there had to be some way we could connect with it in an embodied manner. I then discovered the spiritual research of Slovenian artist and healer Marko Pogacnik. He is truly remarkable, as he has painstakingly observed our subtle energy bodies. He relates how our subtle energies reside at specific bodily locations, or gateways. Using these body locations with intent, we can direct our subtle energies to qualities, or forces, in the Earth's etheric field. Marko has devised and evolved a series of exercises that use these gateways to forge loving links with our living Earth. He called these exercises Gaia Touch. When we make an effort to link our subtle bodies with the Earth, he believes she benefits. He also believes that the time is ripe for us to develop these latent faculties. We must consciously connect with the Earth as a living entity. In his many books written over the past three decades he has included various exercises. With right intent, his exercises strengthen relations between human beings and the "earthly cosmos". They help us attune to the different dimensions of our planet. There are new realities emerging at various levels. It is all about change, and Gaia Touch exercises help us to adapt.

We will more readily embody new dimensions in the future. It requires active preparing on our part. I embraced all Marko's books. I spent some time collating all his exercises so I could gain a better understanding of his work. The elementals and divine forces that inhabit the subtle dimensions guide his work. They appear to Marko in his waking and dreaming life. Marko emphasizes that everything within the Earth cosmos also expresses itself within the human body. There is no real division between ourselves and the Earth. He perceives the living Earth as imbued with the Christ Essence. This philosophy echoes that of Rudolf Steiner, a spiritual scientist now deceased. This Christian esotericist lived around a hundred years ago. His research influenced many walks of life, including biodynamic farming.

Having studied theology, I believe that Jesus shared his teachings, devoid of dogma. He did not request a religion be set up in his name. Others founded Christianity later, years after he had bodily moved away from Palestine. People like Marko are paving a path that may lie closer to the truth of Jesus' teachings. Marko's thinking continually evolves, mirroring a spiritual growth fuelled by a healthy restlessness. He avoids false divisions between Christianity, paganism or indeed shamanism. Instead he fuses the approaches in a universal holographic approach. This approach has a ring of authenticity for me.

After I first bought one of Marko's books in a local art gallery, I had a strong desire to meet him. I contacted the organizer of an upcoming workshop with him in Germany. She urged me to attend as she was unsure how much longer he was going to lead such workshops, due to his increasing age. The workshop was to be in English as well as German so I set off. Several trains, buses, taxis and a plane ride later I arrived at the conference centre. There was an air of expectancy in the room. Marko arrived, looking a very young senior. At that moment the organizer requested that Jackie Queally stand up. It turned out there were no other non-German speakers and so I was assigned an interpreter! The next day an Icelander grappled with translating everything in hushed tones. Out of sympathy Marko started to speak English too. Whenever it came to questions though, I was the only one who had any. I was full of them. The workshop evolved into a sort of protracted English interview. This seemed to please everyone. Marko came forward at the end to thank me for all my insights! He vowed to travel to Ireland one day as he had always felt a pull to the Burren where I live. A few years later, we held an international workshop in the Burren.

My spiritual background had been in synergy light work. This involved the direct experiencing of "Metatronic energies". These emanate from a very divine energy field overseen by the archangel Metatron. Humans can only expose themselves to such high emanations for short periods. I found Marko's approach to spiritual (or non-physical) dimensions refreshing and grounding. He embraced and discerned energies that resided on a whole range of levels. He would rather not concern himself with high dimensions alone. He said we had to be able to work with many realities that were within our grasp when working in groups. Marko shared his current dreams and visions at the workshop. They informed me that he was operating at Metatronic levels too. I shared my own interpretations based on my understanding of Metatronic light codes. The sharing seemed to help him move through a process quicker. I perceive symbols as evidence of a co-creative process between many spiritual agencies. I had learnt about these symbols, or light codes, from a seasoned mystic, William Buehler. All indeed is One. Marko's speciality was to find ways to clear the land from pain and stuck energy. He strove to work from a neutral loving space that does not project any human states of disharmony.

I grappled for some months after the workshop to contextualize my experiences. It had been my pattern to align with the highest light spectrum available to humankind. Whenever I was outside in nature I surrendered to that dimension effortlessly. Marko had explained that we were not only spiritual beings but also human beings. We have to care for one another and for nature's beings. Sometimes humans need healing of trauma so that they can assimilate higher frequencies. It was out of compassion for his fellow human being that he researched new ways of being.

His more recent books indicate that he realizes that the Earth does not need healing. It is rather that we have a role in helping Gaia transmute. She, alongside ourselves, is entering entirely new dimensions. We do not need to impose healing on the Earth. Instead, we witness the core essence of a place from a state of love not fear. This co-creates a new reality by moving the silence, or pre-sound, that underpins all life. I certainly find that true.

Back in Ireland, with Marko's blessing, I ran a short series of classes based on his exercises. I then ran occasional days outside to practise them on the land. People reported feeling great peace and joy, which often lasted for days. In the meantime, Marko went on to become the International

Artist for Peace with UNESCO. This role fostered his ability to engender peace, in collaboration with the elementals. Marko would say if you have done the exercises correctly, you will find peace as an aftermath of doing them. This reminds me of when I used to lead groups in synergy light work. Participants always felt a deep peace afterwards. This is a highly natural state of being and the expected response to the work. It is a bi-product of engaging in authentic spiritual work. From my earlier experiences in synergy light work I could appreciate how Gaia Touch also works with universal light codes. It prepares us for the new incoming co-creative energies. When we engage in such service we find our own personal and spiritual development is boosted automatically.

Another summer came around, and I started to include Gaia Touch when appropriate in my day tours. I also incorporated them into dowsing workshops and I found people responded favourably. Then in the Spring of 2016 Marko visited with a group of fellow Slovenians. I managed to gather 36 people from Ireland and Europe for a special workshop in the Burren. This is a unique geological area in Counties Clare and Galway in the west of Ireland. The aim was to release the Sidhe, or high elementals, from their Europe-wide retreat in the Burren. After gaining a good grounding of the exercises at the workshop I worked with Marko a few times in Ireland. Now I have adapted many of them to incorporate at sites I visit myself. Guests tried out the exercises as a means of reconnecting with nature, and the results were great. That Autumn I was invited to Nova Scotia, Canada where I included some of the many exercises in my Celtic Tree workshops. I found using the Gaia Touch exercises helped our work with trees, and opened people up to new dimensions. Trees are the oldest settlers on the planet, and they have the capacity to recall their origins. They come from an earlier Paradise on Earth. I have sensed their magic myself but have not had the presence of mind to articulate this quality. As Marko so aptly puts it, trees exude beauty, purity, peace and love. Forests create a network of subtle energy spheres for beings to inhabit.

At the time of writing this book I started to lead walks around the dates of the eight Celtic festivals (see Chapter 7). I select areas where we can reconnect with the trees growing there, and use Gaia Touch as one way of doing so. I first led a Winter Solstice walk along the river Inagh in Ennistymon West Clare. This is where my ancestors are buried, and coincidentally there have been many "signs" that I am doing this work for the ancestors.

Please bear in mind that the exercises work with areas of the body that correspond to cosmic forces. For instance, each of our fingers connects with a different dimension of the Earth, as well as a major element. Each human chakra, or energy centre, has a correspondent elemental chakra point in our bodies too.

There is a polarity between our back and front space, or between our causal and manifest worlds. We work on both in tandem in the exercises. Fear is what blocks our flow between causal and manifest worlds. We tend to try to artificially control our world, and as a result suffocate the elementals, who have a natural role and purpose within our world. They could support us in our endeavours if we were more sensitive to their presence. Whenever we suffer trauma and blockages, our psychological armour rears up. We each have a personal elemental being who when we are under stress can no longer reach our organs. Then disease can set in.

Marko trusted the invisible beings of nature to reveal to him the true identity of a place. These beings are always contributing to the life forces in the Earth. They informed his exercises on a deep level.

Every site visited will have its own community of elementals. They may require adaptation of the exercises. People should perform them with imagination and an understanding of the specific purpose.

I am very grateful to both William Buehler and Marko Pogacnik. They have shared so much so freely with me. It leads me to share some of the exercises I feel are pertinent when working with trees.

Exercise to Detect the Magic of a Forest

Movement 1

Stand and look with a soft gaze upon the forest scene ahead of you. Can you see movement? Listen to every leaf moving and any sounds. Can you smell anything? Can you feel air upon your skin? How does it feel standing in this direction? Then turn clockwise a quarter turn and look again. Repeat this until you turn eight times in all, and have returned to your original direction. Observe how you feel.

Movement 2
Now repeat the movements but do not turn one quarter turn each time. Instead, turn very slowly round, without stopping. This time, how does it differ? I find that the focus shifts, making it easier to sense the causal side of life. When the vista is open, long distant views come more into focus when you continually turn around. It can give you a sense of being part of a greater whole when you make this double movement.

Here are some great exercises to help you connect more deeply with the trees:

Stand and breathe as a tree
Imagine you are standing as a tree does in the forest. Strong roots are growing below your feet. Imagine them holding you fast to the ground. Their forces lead deep down into the core of the earth. Above you are the branches leading up to the starry filaments from whence you came. Their forces go to the heart of the universe far from here. Breathe up from the core of the earth into your feet and let the breath travel up and out your head towards the heavens. Pause before taking an in-breath from the heavens into your body. Let it pass out through the soles of your feet into the core of the earth again. Pause before taking a new in-breath and leading it up through your body once more as you begin the cycle again. Repeat this a few times and observe how you feel.

Facing a tree with your Back
Turn your back to the tree and try to sense it with your back. Your back hosts the elemental side of your body where you can empathize with nature more readily.

Tail exercise
Place your hands behind your back and let your middle fingers touch. Point your hand downwards into your backspace, pointing toward the earth. Imagine the hands are following the line of your spine extended, as if you had a tail. You can tilt your pelvis to emphasize the downward direction of your tail if you wish.

Connect your essence with the tree. This gesture shows the tree your animal side and encourages it to reveal its elemental aspect to you. Imagining you have a tail can heighten your sense of the tree you are directing your attention to.

Directing your senses

Trees are the 'primeval daughters of Gaia'. Can you sense a tree's power in your body when you look directly at it? It is a power that comes from deep within the earth, from the very core of the planet. Somehow the trees act as conduits for this primeval energy.

Stand and visualize a column of light inside you. It leads from the centre of earth to your crown. A tree too is connected like this. Now connect with the essence of a tree and become one with it. Extend yourself over the whole area its crown reaches. Sense the unity of the place and its unique energy.

The following exercises are from *Universe of the Human Body* written by Marko Pogacnik. Full permission was granted.

To Perceive the Essence of a Plant or Tree

1. Stand in front of your chosen plant. Communicate that you are approaching it from the level of your heart. If the plant is small, kneel or sit in front of it rather than stand.
2. Show your intent to the plant by pointing your hands toward your heart.

3. Immediately afterwards turn your hands toward the plants with an opening gesture.
4. Return your hands toward your heart with the same gesture as in No. 2. Imagine you are taking the essence of the plant into your heart.
5. Repeat this back and forth a few times, so that the plant can notice it. Be present in a loving way.
6. Become still and listen to the plant. If needed, repeat the exercise after awhile.

The Healing Tear of Grace

1. Lift your hands in prayer gesture to the level of your heart. Let a drop of your compassion fall into the space between your hands.
2. Bow to the earth and reach deep with your hands into the realm of Gaia, the Mother of Life. Create a vessel with your hands and ask Gaia for a drop of her forgiveness. This can be for any distress or insult done to the place or its beings.
3. Straighten up, lifting your hands with the drop of your compassion and the drop of Gaia's forgiveness. Raise the vessel to the heavens and ask for the tear of Sophia's grace.

4. The healing elixir is now collected. Guide the vessel toward the object or preconceived goal. Keep a firm heart connection with the chosen tree in this instance. Ask all its invisible spirit beings to accompany the gift of grace on its way. Continue for a while to be present there through the vibration of your heart.
5. Give thanks.

To Transform the elemental forces of the Earth into the creative impulses of the Human

1. Stand and reach into your back space with your hands. Bring them together behind you; middle fingers are touching. There you establish contact with the primeval or elemental forces within your body. They are in a sphere-like structure.
2. Guide your hands laterally up your body. Let the middle fingers of your hands touch again on front of your chest and throat region.
3. As you move your arms upwards, bow your head backward so as to liberate your throat.
4. With your head bowed back, create a circle in front of your throat with your hands. Now the primeval forces of Gaia are being transformed into creative powers. These forces are akin to the dragon energies.

5. After a while open your hands and stretch them out. This enables the creative powers to flow out into the environment, where they can support the creative processes of the planet.
6. Guide the arms laterally down your body and straighten up your head ready to repeat the exercise.
7. Repeat the exercise a few times and then rest for awhile with closed eyes, to sense what is happening in your body.

I suggest doing the above exercise before people connect personally with the forces of a tree. It helps them respond creatively to it. I use the Healing Tear of Grace on any tree that has suffered natural or manmade destruction. After the exercise it is good to dowse the effects; normally its aura will have vastly strengthened.

It is important to allow yourself time to feel the effects of all the exercises.

Chapter 7

Festival Walks

Now I would like to present an example of how we can incorporate both Gaia Touch and toning. Slow walks in nature are conducive to the exercises. The following walk occurred on a Winter Solstice in Ennistymon in County Clare.

It is important to allow yourself time to feel the effects of the exercises.

Winter Solstice Walk

Following a talk I gave, people asked me to organise a Winter Solstice Walk. The river Inagh shares its name with a mythical river goddess. She rushes through my ancestral village, forming picturesque rapids near its old stone bridge. We met inside the local community centre before setting off. Most people had not encountered Gaia Touch and so we practiced them a little at first.

Then we gathered on the lawn outside the Falls Hotel, where we could see the old church and cemetery on the opposite hill. The hotel is built over a previous castle site. I often wonder if the cemetery was once a fort. These two high points act like twin towers, overlooking the river cascades.

Circle Gathering

We started in a circle with a few simple Gaia touch exercises to connect with our ancestors. I was aware of my own ancestors buried on the hill. The Midwinter Solstice is a great time to honour our ancestors. At this time of year, darkness will increase no more. The light will return as the season turns. How fitting to stand in a landscape so harmoniously balanced, bisected by a goddess river!

Honouring the Trees

Then we followed the river downstream to where it shortly turned into a beautiful small glen or dell. This was where the winter solstice walk was to take place. En route we noted how the trees dramatically hugged the steep banks, or arched over the river. We paused to do an exercise to perceive the essence of some remarkable trees. After we shared our experiences we each silently expressed gratitude for the trees. It was obvious that the trees were touching our hearts and minds. As we entered the glen, I spotted a small tree that a storm had struck. We first dowsed the tree's energy field. We then performed the exercise I often use with trees that are hurting, The Healing Tear of Grace. I then took out my tuning forks and selected a couple of combinations of notes for the group to tone to the tree. First we dispersed its pain and we used harmonies to balance it again. Dowsing revealed its aura greatly expanded. Some people sensed a lot of gratitude from the tree.

The Sun Blessing

We walked to the very end of the path where a tree had fallen across the banks. Someone spotted a lighted candle in a mossy nook beside where we stood. This felt like a blessing on our work. Pausing on the footbridge we did a silent exercise to take our old world and project it into the new world beyond. We wished to transform the energies of the old year into the New Year, which in our imagination lay upstream. Choosing the concave arch of a huge tree to pause at, I rang my set of tinsha bells to ring in the new. As the bells touched, the sun came out in full pelt upon the spot. From there on the sun seemed to emerge from the clouds each time we stopped to do an exercise. It was magical (and cold!).

Toning the Chakras

Now we started our journey into rebirth. We toned the base chakra note and vowel sound before setting off from the bridge.

We toned the sacral chakra where the river ran into a narrow channel that resembled the birth canal.

We also did an exercise to help the elementals in their work. This keyed into the sacrum, which is the seat of our personal elementals.

We then entered a strong elemental area, where miniature fairy-like houses had formed among the mossy banks and tree roots. Witches' broom grew in profusion, which can be an indicator of a strong fairy presence. We formed a circle and connected with the middle, lower and upper worlds. Once again, the sun burst out as we gathered around. Here I sensed was the area of the Solar Plexus Chakra.

Animals Empathize

A dog ran through us without any fuss. Its owner remarked that this was most unusual. Animals can sense when humans are acting in harmony with nature. I chose a small island for the heart chakra toning, and again someone sighted a nice coincidence. A heart-shaped leafed plant was growing by our feet. This belonged to a prematurely growing celandine.

For the throat chakra, I chose an exercise that transforms archetypal energies into creative processes. This action is important for our current year. We can block our creativity through negative responses to our external world. Now more than ever we need to use our imaginations.

Envoys of Peace

Finally at the crown chakra area, we toned. Then we renewed the fairy essence within the human being in a beautiful exercise. We imagined a pair of butterfly wings growing from behind each one of us. Then we imagined the butterfly transforming into a white bird of peace. We sent these birds flying from our elemental hearts (at the top of the sternums). The birds flew over long reeds that shroud the Inagh on her way to sea in Liscannor Bay. We imagined them reaching the angelic realms that lay beyond our view.

Eager to continue, we made a circle and repeated our group exercise, even playing with it a little. This stimulated our heart energy! Feeling whole, invigorated, yet decidedly cold, we set off for town. Ennistymon has delightful coffee houses and art galleries. As I left, I was already anticipating a similar trip for Imbolc in early February!

Chapter 8

DOWSING

I HAVE MENTIONED THE ART OF dowsing in relation to both sound and Gaia Touch exercises with trees. You can use a simple set of dowsing rods made from bent wire (old coat hangers are useful), or a pendulum. You can use these dowsing tools to get answers on a whole host of applications. I have used them in personal healing sessions, remote dowsing of maps, and finding ley lines at sites.

In this instance we are using them to measure the energy fields of trees. Once someone showed me how there are spirit doorways on the trunks of trees. I found this quite interesting. First, let's establish what movement represents your positive and also your negative. Hold the rods loosely in your fists. Keeping them parallel with the ground, ask a question to which you know the answer is yes and next ask a question that requires a no answer. Observe the movement of the rods. For instance, the rods may cross together for a positive and swing apart for a negative answer. If you use a pendulum, it may swing to and fro, or swing anti-clockwise or clockwise for your negative. It should swing the opposite way or go to and fro for your positive. Holding your rod or pendulum, ask again for it to show you its Yes and No responses, using closed questions that you know the answer is a definite Yes or No. With repeated practice you can see how your tool responds. Once you feel confident you can interpret the Yes and No, you are ready to use the tool to measure energy fields.

Approach your tree to communicate with it via sound or a Gaia Touch exercise. First measure the energy field of the tree. Approach the tree from at least a few meters away from its trunk and ask it to show you the edge of its first energy field. There may be several rings of energy round a tree, look for the one closest to the trunk, to avoid confusion here. Walk slowly and steadily toward the tree, with rods held one in each hand, parallel to the ground. If you are using a pendulum set it to a gentle swing. As you near the tree, there should be a definite turning of the rods or increase of movement of the pendulum. This demonstrates a definite shift in energy as it encounters the edge of an auric field. Make sure you test for energies all the way right up to the trunk in case the tree has a very shrunken aura. You may be able to pick up its energy naturally and then you can view dowsing as an external prop.

The auric fields encircle the tree. At times the tree is not in the centre of the circle but to one side, or the circle is flattened. Group toning is often more effective than just one person administering the tones. After spending some time toning beside a selected tree, try testing the effects of the exercise. Make sure you step back further as you approach the tree, as the energy field may have grown larger. People often find the energy field has at least doubled in size. You can also vary the exercise by accompanying it with focused intent or without. You can test by dowsing to see how your focus impacts on the energy field. If comparing with and without using intent, this will take time, as you have to allow the tree to neutralize first. It may be best to mark the spot of the rings and return after a walk or a break and repeat it. In time you will become confident of your ability to measure your impact on the tree.

The exercises in dowsing can show that we can communicate on subtle levels with the trees. Everything links to one another in the etheric worlds where our thoughts and intents lay. By dowsing in nature, we can slow down and take note of our precious surrounds. This in itself is a healing activity.

The beauty of the methods I have shared so far is their simplicity. They do not need a long, vigorous spiritual training. This sharply contrasts with our Celtic predecessors.

Chapter 9

THE KNOWLEDGE CONTINUUM

IN THIS FINAL CHAPTER, I offer some of the ideas I have floated around for many years. Some of the information is academic while other is speculative and popular. It is up to the reader to decide what the truth may be. However it may be useful to certain readers to have a more left-brained chapter on the way that the Celtic Trees connect with other spiritual groups and so forth.

To begin, the Druids are said to have asked the defeated race for knowledge, which the Druids incorporated into their own esoteric practices. This was apparently at the end of the Bronze Age, when the rule of the Tuatha De Danaan was coming to an end. A somewhat mythical race, the Tuatha either literally or metaphorically went underground. The Druids replaced the land with a more masculine-oriented society, based on the extensive use of iron.

Origins of Ogham

Legend says that Pythagoras in the sixth century BC studied with the Druids in the north. He claimed the far north held the greatest wisdom. (It was perhaps the Outer Hebrides, where Callanish and several more circles of stones once stood). There are also archival murmurings of ancient connections between Ireland and Egypt. If it is true, we can imagine the following scenario. Shortly after a great flood took place, civilization would have regrouped. A long oral tradition in the northwest of Europe developed. It managed to preserve kernels of Atlantean ancient knowledge. This knowledge survived the centuries, held in remote island communities overseen by Druids. Thus Pythagoras encountered these Druids on his travels, and found true inspiration in their teachings. It is clear that trees held distinctive inner qualities that the Druids revered. They worked with a mysterious finger (dactyl) alphabet perhaps based on the initial sound of each tree. This was the Ogham.

The alphabet may have concealed a cosmology and philosophy. The Ogham ordering of letters perhaps explored the natural world and man's relation to it. The Druids deciphered the messages of the trees. They underwent great preparations to do this. They had to develop their powers of imagination to a great extent. However, Druidic initiation was conducted in secret, without leaving records.

In the Celtic Legend cycles there is mention of the god Ogma. His name gave rise to the Ogham alphabet:

"From whence, what time, and what person, and from what place, did the Ogham spring?"
"The place is Hibernia, which we Scots inhabit; in the time of Breass the son of Elathan, then king of Ireland. The person was Ogma, son of Elathan, brother to Breass, for Breass, Ogma and Delva were three sons of Elathan. Ogma was a man much skilled in dialects and in poetry. It was he who invented the Ogham. Its object was to create signs of secret speech only known to the learned, and designed to be kept from the vulgar…"

The above information comes from a late fourteenth century Irish annul. Ogma (pronounced Oma) is also mentioned in Irish legends. He belonged to the tribe of gods named the Tuatha de Danaan, who inhabited the fairy realms. They ruled the land with supernatural power. Some scholars place Ogma as having lived around 1000 BC, and some place him earlier.

It is also interesting to note the mention of the Scots in the above quotation from the Book of Ballymote. A subdivision of that tribe settled in Scotland, giving Scotland its present name. Some say the Picts used their own form of glyphs. There is speculation that theirs is an even older form of Ogham, whose meaning has been lost. Its magic was more potent and undiluted. The Scotti glyphs are etched on standing stones, and only an elite few were ever versed in reading them. Modern academia struggle with doing so. It is possible that the originators of the glyphs knew the Ogham could impart a message to even the uninitiated observer. It may have worked at an energetic level. Perhaps they imbued the letters with energies by creating them with intent.

The Ogham as we know them today may not have been the original sacred glyphs. It is possible that the Ogham was introduced in the Bronze Age by a mysterious race that took over Ireland. In the Boyne Valley, there are Ogham inscriptions of the birch and yew at the prehistoric portal of Newgrange. These represent aspects of life and death respectively. This would indeed suggest a very early usage of Ogham. The evidence suggests that the Druids preserved an already established Ogham. Druids, bards and healers incorporated the Ogham into their own secret practices. It contained magical properties and even spiritual powers. It is believed that the Ogham were also used for divining purposes.

There may have been more ancient markings in the Stone Age that did not adhere to any homogenous system. As the signs evolved, the Celts adapted them into their own blueprint alphabet. This was during their Golden Age of creativity. The Beth-Luis-Nion alphabet used in the Ogham Calendar is believed by some to have grown out of the ancient finger language. Since the Druids orally passed on secrets of these encoded glyphs in private initiations, we do not know much about the historical significance and origins of the Ogham. The notion of written sounds may have spread from the east, as Irish legends attest to. In the Bronze Age vigorous trade ensued between Ireland and the Mediterranean region. This might have influenced the Druids to create their own written records of their words. A nineteenth century translation of a work by Abubekr bin Wahshih in 800 CE is worth noting. It effectively links the Ogham with old writing of the east. It noted that Plato's alphabet was grouped into a series of five characters with similar patterning of strokes to the Ogham. There is reference to two alphabets: "One is Plato's alphabet and the other belonged to Dioscorides the philosopher. It was commonly called the Tree Alphabet".

Irish may have imported their knowledge of the Ogham from their travels in the east. Or perhaps they invented it themselves and took it to ancient Greece. The Irish Ogham appears the most sophisticated alphabet of the early examples. So this suggests the Druids brought their knowledge to the Greeks at some point. Other historical evidence held in Cork, Ireland, indicates the Ogham carried a resemblance to an alphabet found in Thebes. The ancient bards of Ireland recited that their ancestors came from the east. However, this does not mean to say they originated in the east as the Hibernians used to travel a good deal. An examination of ancient Egyptian alphabets may reveal some correlation with the Ogham. There exist legendary migrations from Egypt to Ireland. Myths can allude to various stages of consciousness in the evolution of mankind. This indigenous alphabet seemed to arise from the depth of man's soul in the west. It requires a renewed strength of imagination to penetrate the minds and souls of our ancestors.

The Celtic calendar represents tree species that still proliferate today. It offers an ideal springboard for such work of the imagination.

The physical ordering of the Ogham

It is interesting to note that there are 150 different types of Ogham script with 360 examples found in Ireland and Britain. The majority are in Ireland, particularly in the southwest. There are only a few in Scotland. There were four main categories of trees in the system. The chieftains were the most respected group, occupying the highest strata:

- chieftain or noble
- peasant
- shrub
- bramble

The Culdees

From the outset I would like to point out that I choose not to make false divisions between people. For instance, I don't appreciate the labels Paganism and Christianity. I have always held an interest in the Culdees, a group of early Christian monks and priests. They were both male and female. Their stories suggested they were very sensitive to earth energies. Often their miracles were reminiscent of Shamanic practices. Theirs was a form of Christianity that stemmed from the Middle East, established during the time of international tin and copper trading in Britain and Ireland. The early Coptic church shares its roots in symbolism with the Celts and many motifs can be found on high crosses and other stones in Ireland still. This stage of history established one of many links with Egypt across time. The "Dysart" or "desert" settlements of early Christians in parts of Britain and especially southern Ireland tell of that tradition in the name. From my personal research I believe there was a body of fleeing Essenes from Egypt and surrounding areas that sailed to Ireland and Britain for refuge. Greek and Roman travel writers reported their presence here as early as 37 A.D. (Isobel Hill Elder 1937 *Celt, Druid and Culdee*). Moreover the Culdees worked with local Pagan beliefs, much in the same way that Christianity worked in parts of Africa to blend their religion with that of the indigenous people. Certainly the Culdees' respect and love for nature would have extended into honouring the trees.

The Roman Church started to phase out Culdee beliefs and practices from the mid-seventh century onwards. This commenced with the Synod of Whitby in north England. Dogma and religion gradually precluded a nature-based spirituality. Yet the universal truths held by these early Christians prevailed. They remained in small, somewhat fringe Christian circles and movements. Wherever the Roman Church loosens its influence on society, spirituality and inclusivity returns. Even with the Roman Church, a more all-embracing set of beliefs is beginning to emerge. I personally believe the Christ event carried great cosmic significance. It has enabled us to become more consciously aware of our divinity. When we become aware of the possibility for non-conditional love, this can be linked to spirituality or religion. I call this love the Christ essence and I see it as a universal energy, as do many healers. It seems that humanity is awakening more and more to the impulse of this far-reaching love. The coming of the Christ harkened an awakening to our own divinity which we are only realizing now.

Meanwhile, what of our natural world? Ancient Culdee thought placed Christ consciousness at the centre of both the nature realm and the human realm. Both realms were inter-connected. This body of thought still holds true today. A follower of the works of mystic Rudolf Steiner, Eleanor Merry in *The Flaming Door* 1938 wrote: "Christ's presence was felt in the elements long before he came. Earlier still, it was felt in the world of the stars." The perceived wisdom behind the creation of the universe now transformed into a tangible energy. It became love, felt in the souls of initiates as they beheld their beloved trees.

There is a deep universal love present in nature, particularly in our trees. It is the elementals that create the space for this love to flourish. Nature draws on a pool of all-encompassing love. She carries an awareness that is more attuned to the future than we as humans are. That is why plant essences can help people become more focused on their soul purpose. Also being in nature can help us focus our thoughts.

Poems such as Merddyn's (aka Merlin's) bardic lament from the Scottish Borders hint of the role that trees played. It suggests that the trees were the main communicators of a holy presence at the time. In the remains of a late fifteenth century manuscript entitled "Lailoken and Kentigern" we read of a Scottish Merlin figure who lamented:

> "I am neglected by my former friends, and wander among skeptics who know me not…Thou sweet an beneficent tree! Not scanty is the fruit with which thou art loaded, but upon thy account I am terrified and anxious lest the woodsman should come, those profaners of the wood, to dip they root and corrupt the seed that no apple may ever grow upon thee more. Upon me Gwenddoleu freely bestowed these precious gifts: but he is, this day, as if he had never been".

Sacred Geometry

The qualities of the trees fitted within a pattern that connected them to one another and to a cosmic whole. When plotted as a circular calendar, they form a geometrical pattern. It is as if the Druids saw behind creation, to the very thought forms. These formed themselves into a world of natural beauty.

In the late 1990s I condensed a vast body of research I had gathered on the Celtic Trees into a slim poetry book. I entitled it *Tree Murmurs*. The Celtic Tree Calendar, as devised by Robert Graves, is based on a set of trees indigenous to the UK and Ireland. In *Tree Murmurs*, I inserted a diagram outlining the cycle of the seasons as viewed in the Celtic period. The "vowel trees" represent the five main seasons within the Celtic Year. It included two harvest periods. These seasons form a pentagram around which the thirteen lunar months in Grave's Celtic calendar can be placed. Those trees whose names begin with consonants include two of which are double consonants. I then superimposed the eight major Celtic Festivals and noted the resultant geometric pattern. This posed a striking resemblance to symbolism used by the later Knights Templar.

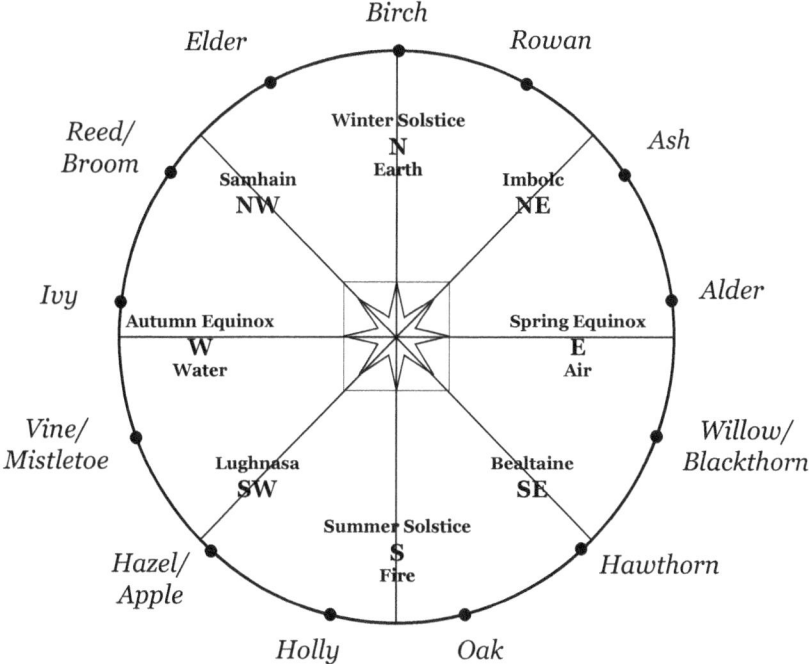

The Lunar Year with its seasonal cohorts, consonants and vowels

The eight major Celtic festivals take up each of the eight directions. These occur at the eight corners formed by the two overlapping squares in the above diagram. The Celtic festivals followed the path of the Sun in the sky. In contrast the thirteen lunar months represent thirteen lunar cycles. The god Ogma had a strong association with the sun. The interplay of the sun and the moon is a strong feature of the Ogham ordering of letters.

The Eight Directions

The Templar cross also demarcated eight points. Each of the four arms of the Templar cross has two pointed corners, creating eight points in total. These also relate to the eight directions albeit on a more esoteric level.

Templar cross

Many indigenous tribes throughout the world speak of four cardinal directions. When you insert the diagonal directions, they represent the cross-quarterly festivals. In Celtic culture these start with Imbolc in Spring. They tend to be more inward and highly charged in quality, and are associated with strong deities. I always pay attention to the cross-quarterlies. Let me explain why.

I am influenced by a large body of experiential knowledge called the Reshel. I learnt this from an esteemed mystic who wrote to me daily for many years. William Buehler from Crestone, Colorado taught me much about Templar symbolism that seems closely linked with the Reshel. Following a distinguished Naval career, ex-Commander Buehler had become a scholar of ancient Hebrew. It revealed to him a sacred language which he called the Reshel. He was able to identify the different energy bodies that emanate from one divine source. William conducts ongoing independent research into early Hebrew and the proto-Sinaitic glyphs, which he views as descriptors for a synergic process of creation.

While William uses right-brain thinking to investigate the dimensions where these codes originate, he also has a wealth of spiritual experiences to draw upon. Since the 1970s William has exposed himself on a regular basis to "synergy light work". Buehler still today conducts this specialist light work with a view to moving the silence, or "Selah", in Hebrew. By leaving our time/space continuum for brief periods the group exposes themselves to "Metatronic" dimensions that are overseen by a very high archangel called Metatron. In each session the light group members are able to make contact with a far more divine universe. Such a dimension naturally contrasts with our own three-dimensional world. In William's estimation we are rapidly returning to this "full light spectrum". There, co-creation is possible, due to cosmic energies available to us in this window of time. Until I actually participated in this work I was not able to fully realize its rare quality, nor its implications. Since humans are separated from the Source, its divine presence is perceived in symbols and other phenomena, which flood in during one of these sessions in synergy light work.

Much of William's work concerned the Templar codes of co-creation. William realized that there was an inner core of Templars whose visions of the higher dimensions fed into their symbols that are visible in cathedrals, burial marker stones, and early heraldry. The idea of creating, or realizing, Heaven on Earth was one of the core purposes of the Knights Templar. It was the spiritual motive behind the inner core of Templars. I have no doubt that an inner sanctum of Knights Templar was working with this dynamic at Rosslyn Chapel in Scotland. I was able to transfer William's knowledge to the stone carvings still present at Rosslyn Chapel in Scotland, where I was the first external guide. William explained how their carvings of diagonal crosses signified a mutable cross. Switching over the cardinal points to the diagonals creates a dynamic movement. It symbolizes a connection with higher dimensions. These are not fixed in our time-space continuum! An eight armed cross best describes this process, but the shorthand version would be a diagonal cross.

He determined that our eight directions link into a higher reality plane of existence. In that realm, spiritual programmes continually unfold. His analysis of the eight directions has proved invaluable over the years. I have witnessed the eight directions in ley lines in temples and cathedrals, particularly those constructed by the Knights Templar. They were the last group en masse to use the knowledge.

Given that many Templar sites were earlier occupied by Celtic monks, we should perhaps look to their "logo" too. It was an equal armed wide cross. The earlier Celtic cross hints at the eight points but not as clearly as in the Templar cross. There seems to be a progression of knowledge signified by the two crosses. The Celtic hermits reached deep states in meditation, reaching high angelic frequencies. The Templars achieved similar high states of being in their synergic efforts.

I believe that the Druids likewise were able to build a collective knowledge of their trees that reflected the co-creative energies extant in the higher realms of being. Rosslyn Chapel, south of Edinburgh, illustrates this knowledge of trees and plants in its many carvings that are intertwined with the angelic and human realms. The chapel also incorporated the eight directions in its layout with appropriate carvings to illustrate their meaning. Let us look at the eight directions inherent in the geometry of the Celtic Calendar. I will portray how the eightfold aspect of directions represents this more rarified and holy universe.

Here are the chief qualities for each of the eight solar directions. I will consider them from both a human and "Metatronic" viewpoint.

Northeast

We start with the northeast, as the highest spiritual energies first enter from the northeast. They set the tone of their mission. It is the reason why heel stones were placed to the northeast of powerful ancient henges, such as Stonehenge. Likewise certain cathedrals such as Chartres in France were oriented northeast. Foundation stones in the northeast of powerful medieval chapels illustrate the dynamic, such as in Rosslyn Chapel in Scotland.

By starting at a quarterly point, we set up a mutable cross system. This generates a dynamic and evolving energy field. If we started in the North, we would be working with a fixed cross system. This cannot move so readily to embrace new energies.

Redemptive powers flow into the earth in the northeast. The divine energies enter the living Earth/Gaia here, aligning with purity. It links the light to universal love. Illumination is possible. The Earth is long associated with the perfect Mother/Goddess/Queen. She carries the potential from the universe and beyond within her, and gives birth to a new divine being now.

The Celtic traditional fire festival of Imbolc is placed here. The Elm or Pine Season brings love, purification, wisdom and light. Other elements enter with the lunar trees of the Rowan and Ash. These offer great promise for success. Also the notion of polarities enters with the Ash. This indicates a process where the Spirit of One begins to divide into a denser vibration.

East

At this point in the solar year there is equal light and darkness. It is placed at one pole of an event plane/event horizon or "teleplane", out of which matter manifests. In shamanic practices it is seen as moon-glint on water. There are other symbols for this phenomenon. This pole is the female pole whose purpose is to manifest from spirit into the material world. That is why the Spring Equinox is associated with fertility and the female goddess. The female aspect nurtures and prepares the complex patterns of creation within. She prepares the way for the single male action to be executed. In other words, this point brings spirit into matter.

The Spring Equinox is also associated with creating karma, marking the entrance of the young adult. This is the domain of the Gorse Season, when the warrior prince is in training. The Alder as a lunar tree supports this role.

Southeast

This is where the Tree of Knowledge is placed esoterically. Like the Holy Grail, it is the object of much physical and mental searching. The Path of the Mother goes from the northwest to the southeast. It can be traced in a long ley line over the Earth. The ley starts in the waters off Sligo in Ireland, close to the island of Inismurray. Here legend has it that St. Molaise mentored and gave confession to St. Columba, a natural geomancer, explorer and diplomat. The ley ends at Mount Sinai in Egypt.

Beltaine, the second fire festival of the Celtic year, is placed here on the diagram. This is the domain of the divine Man, often depicted mythically as a warrior prince. It is the season of the tough courageous Gorse. Willow and Blackthorn as lunar trees support this energy. The Blackthorn as a double consonant cleanses deep karmic issues. It enables you to proceed on your path. Fear is not to be courted now. The hawthorn tree too blesses our route to success in manifestation. Expect the yang quality of fire to dominate this season, where an element of risk features strongly.

South

This connects most efficiently with the Sidhe, or Lower Heavens, that reside within our blessed planet. On Midsummer's Day the lid is lifted to the Otherworld, or devic world, that the Sidhe inhabit and Midsummer madness prevails. This is a day that does not belong to any of the lunar months. Now the Summer Solstice is celebrated, when the Sun is at its most potent. The holly brings totally new energy and is often associated with the Christ being. On Midsummer's Day, the Holly may yet topple the old Oak, heralding a new cycle of fresh insights.

We need the Sidhe (pronounced "Shee") as much as we need the cosmic angels. These angels of the Earth sustain our life on Earth. After this pivotal day the inward half of the year starts, and wisdom starts to grow.

Southwest

This is the point of the Solarian creation pillar, where great cosmic solar beings dwell. They assist in the evolution of our planet from afar.

The third Celtic fire festival of Lughnasa resides here, named after the god Lugh, the Sun god of harvests. In mythology Lugh lives in Avalon, where he feasts on abundant apples and hazelnuts growing in an eternal orchard. The Hazel and Apple spirits support the Earth and those of us who live on it. They offer us wisdom and glimpses of a Heaven on Earth. This Celtic fire festival is directly opposite Imbolc in our Celtic Year. It is the time for dissolving attachments and gaining wisdom from our experiences. We can shift gears now and work in a multi-dimensional world.

West

This is the other end of the event horizon I mentioned under the East section. This male pole has the opposite function to that of the East. It has to elevate Matter into Spirit once more.

The festival of the Autumn Equinox is celebrated here. It is the peak of the Yin cycle of the Sun. Ruled by the season of the Aspen, it deals with the outer chaos hiding an inner divine order. The Vine or Mistletoe rules this direction and urges us to bear our fate with dignity. The old Crone energy of the Ivy is also within this region. Everything is urging us inward into the growing darkness and stillness. Within the earth itself, there is new movement stirring in the cauldron of silence.

Northwest

Here is the entrance of the divine mother, who instigates the Path of the Mother across to the southeast. We are not at the point of birth yet though, and the path into the Earth has its own secret initiations. In the Celtic tradition the northwest is linked with the Earth, represented by the Mother.

Here at Samhain, the final fire festival of the Celtic year, we connect with dying and death itself. The intensity of the Yew season marks the occasion. The lunar Elder reminds us of the prevalent process of decay and composting. The other lunar trees, the Reed and Broom, perform similar roles. The Reed connects with archiving events. Meanwhile the Broom energy maintains the lineage of the human race.

North

This connects with the angels and upper heavens. It is between death (Yew) and rebirth (Elm). The goddess continues her sovereignty, the birch tree being the main lunar tree. The Midwinter Solstice occurs here, where new directions show up. There is a rising up and strengthening of energies. This is all necessary for the journey though the birth canal that occurs now.

Dimensions of Being

In summarizing the directions I have included some aspects of the Metatronic realms. You can regard them as states of being, rather than physical places. These high vibrations are reaching into our world more and more as the Earth transits into a new state of being. It would be good to view the entire calendar of trees from various dimensions. When you can, spend some time in deep meditation with each of the trees. Such an exercise is valid as the whole of the Earth is upgrading now and we need to prepare. Part of our journey of change involves considering the potential for nature. We often talk about human potential but Nature has her own trajectory to fulfil. With probing we can sense her true divine source.

Let us consider the role of Nature in this collective Ascension process. According to William Buehler, Metatron presides over our universe as the chief archangel. He handles other universes too. Archangel Michael carries the torch for our own planet. This "Metatronic" Universe is a divine one where states of fear, time and space do not exist. We are already in this Metatronic universe when we live in a high vibratory field of love. Nature always exists in this state of being. So it makes sense to view trees and other plants as our pointers to a time when once again Heaven will prevail on Earth. Energetically the trees call in the wisdom from the future and store it for us to tap into if we can.

The Five Vowels

The five season vowel trees form a pentagram, a symbol for the divine feminine. A five pointed star was perceived as a seeding mechanism in Templar symbolism. In other words, it represents an initial thought leading to eventual manifestation.

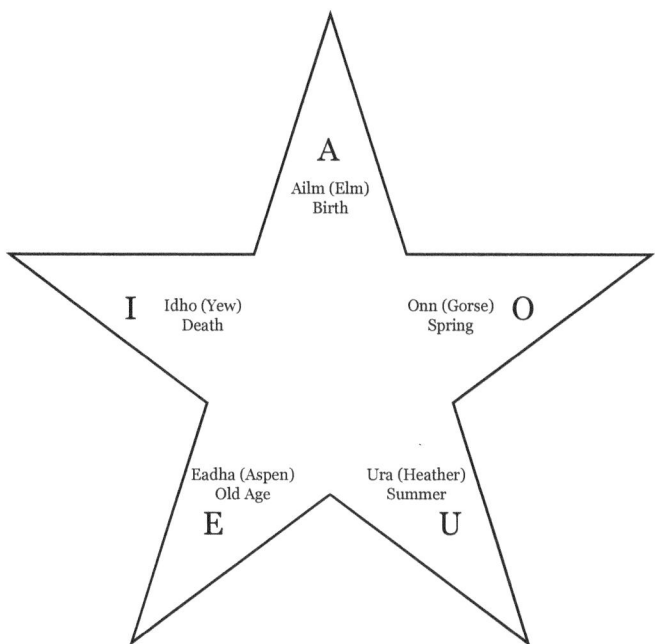

The seasons represented by Vowels in a pentagram

The vowels are less dense than consonants are, for vowels are pure breath. A vowel is created by air, akin to spirit, coming through us unhindered. Each vowel carries a different nuance with it. Our mouth shapes the vowels, with no interference from our tongues, teeth or lips. Compare this to how we sound a consonant, when we have to physiologically intervene in the passage of air. In many ways a vowel can be equated with a more feminine aspect. It is more concerned with feeling than thoughts.

The vowels grease the wheels of the yearly cycle. In contrast the thirteen consonants constitute the nitty-gritty details. They are the denser matter that creates the spinning wheels. They mould our personalities. Form stems from thoughts as represented by the consonants. The vowels colour the consonants in the changing of the seasons. Vowels provide the spiritual setting for form to take place.

Another interpretation of the tree calendar comes from the perspective of Chinese Traditional Medicine (TCM). A few years ago, Ian Claxton, a Galway acupuncturist, approached me after having enjoyed my book *Tree*

Murmurs. He told me he had been inspired to work with the five main vowel trees of the Celtic Tree calendar. Having ordered a company to make essences from these trees, he administered them with his clients. First he experimented with how they may fit into the Five Element theory of TCM (Traditional Chinese Medicine). There is an energy system known to TCM practitioners as the Five Elements, whereby the five main elements either boost or suppress one another. There are twelve meridians or energy pathways in TCM. Each meridian is paired with another so each pair carries a yin and yang quality. The dominant set of characteristics in an individual will indicate which meridian is their constitutional type. Ian fitted the five Celtic vowel trees into the classical Five Element model used in TCM. (No trees represent the sixth pair, the Pericardium/triple warmer.)

You can arrange these five elements in the pentagram as follows:

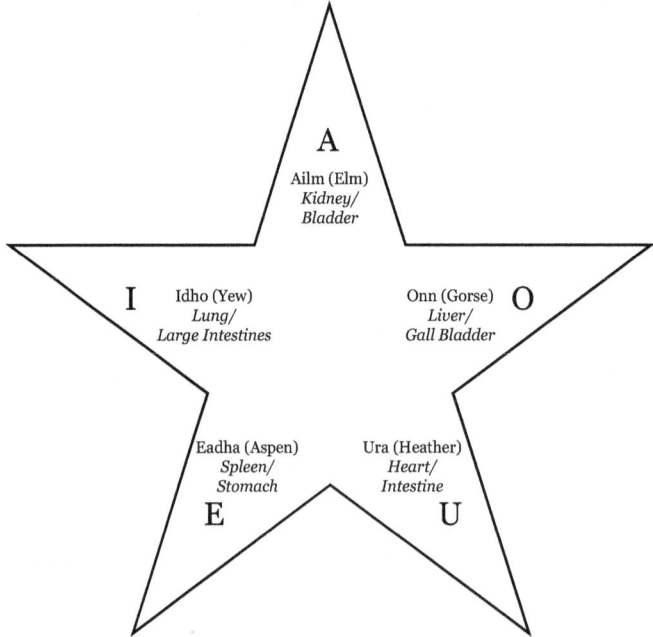

Pentagram to show the five main essences (constitutions) in Ogham Essences

In TCM there is no element for air, although Metal to some extent replaces it. Wood represents another aspect of the air element. It is associated with the pioneering spirit, or new thinking. Perhaps after following all the meditations and reading how the trees relate to one another, you can see how the elements fit well into the tree types. For instance, in the heather season the heart predominates, and this is the time for working with the heart energy. Similarly, the stubborn warrior spirit is allocated in the liver/gall bladder meridian. Ian arranged for essences to be created from these vowel trees. He also ordered essences for each of the thirteen lunar trees. He offered the essences to clients after acupuncture treatment to study the effects. The results were impressive. The lunar essences supported the constitutional remedies of the vowel (seasonal) trees. They were chosen according to the month the essence was administered. I found the concept interesting as I had trained with Fabian Maman who is a sonic acupuncturist. One of the modules I had trained in was the Five Elements in sound healing. Introducing the trees into this theory fascinated me. I attended Ian's first training. Later I found my clients in sound healing benefitted. Many found it shifted inner blockages. They could take the lunar tree either of their birth month or current month.

Taking essences is one way by which you can embrace the energies of a particular tree. I would recommend taking all thirteen essences on a monthly basis for a whole year. This helps you to embrace all aspects in yourself that the various trees will highlight. In these times we need to continually evolve and change, and the plants offer us their loving support to do so. You are welcome to contact me if you wish to have a consultation to ascertain your essence.

The Thirteen Consonants

Let's consider the number thirteen as highlighted by the consonants. The Druids used a thirteen-knot chord in initiations. Within esoteric numerology, the number thirteen signifies instability. Twelve is a stable number, and so we find there are twelve disciples, or twelve knights of the Round Table, and so on. The thirteenth number, or person, introduces an element of instability. It forces the original twelve to regroup, so a new paradigm begins.

By example, within Christianity, Judas Iscariot fulfilled the role of the thirteenth disciple. His role within the twelve disciples was to destabilize the status quo. His actions triggered a series of events that led to a paradigm shift in consciousness. The Crucifixion seeded a more universal love vibration. It is only now coming to fruition. A long period of imposed materialization followed, when Church and State intertwined unhealthily. Organized religions sometimes offered incorrect and insincere interpretations of the Christ message of love.

In esoteric symbolism, the whale/dolphin and the unicorn are the two symbols associated with the energy of the number thirteen. Such motifs were hinted at in the carpet page of that beautiful Celtic manuscript; the Lindisfarne Gospel. In medieval symbolism, Christ was often depicted as the unicorn.

On a micro scale, within the cycle of the natural year, the thirteenth lunar month heralds change and transmutation. In the cycles of the year, if nothing ever changed, we would never have opportunities to evolve. There has to be an unknown force that propels us to move forward. This quality of dynamic movement is highlighted in the solar year by the day of great festivity celebrated at midsummer. It is this Midsummer's Day that allows for the madness that Shakespeare wrote of. It is the foundation material for the new to emerge. Without madness, there is no method!

A Templar Upgrade

When I conduct tours of sacred sites in Scotland they include a lot of material on the Templars. The tours span the period of early Celtic monks through to the Templars. Both the early monks (known as Culdees) and later the Templars used many of the sites we visit. I often got the sense that the Templars upgraded the knowledge carried by the Celtic monks. For the Celts, trees bridged the lower heavens with our human realm. Trees appear to have been a significant cultural factor in their lives. The Culdees revered the Divine Feminine in nature. She was the equal counterpart to the Christ energy available to mankind. The Templars seemed to have performed many spiritual roles, and one of them was to upgrade the Culdee belief system. They revered Mary Magdalene as epitomizing divine femininity. She was the force behind the life manifesting in all processes of Creation. The Templars respected the vast wisdom contained within the realms of nature. Their cathedrals are full of plant carvings honouring her beauty. Their vast pillars have become their trees. The pillars reach from the earth to the cosmos. In these architectural wonders, we are reminded how the lower heavens of earth wisdom are matched by the angelic realms of the wider universe.

The Role of Poetry in upholding the divine in the Human

In medieval times, mathematics (particularly geometry), music and poetry all reflected the divine. Poetry is, in short, the language of the gods. Poetry was traditionally hailed as the human endeavour closest in form to the divine. In New Age terminology, it can carry light codes. For me, when I wish to express the sacred energy of trees, poetry seems the best medium to use.

The bards who spoke in metered prose in Celtic times were held in high esteem. They played a very important spiritual role in society. They were the ones who helped their people form bridges with their divine source. Folk treated their bards with great respect in return. They perceived them as the receptacles for divine energy. This energy was deemed necessary for the well-being of the tribe. Bards acted as the chief advisors to their chieftains, mediating between the cosmic world and the human world. The rulers referred to them in matters of law. Nowadays we could not imagine looking to our rulers for divine guidance! Spin doctors have often replaced our poets. Their messages are hollow and devoid of life-enhancing material. Consciousness has changed, and our divine inspiration is mostly a private matter. Our secular, liberal laws and morals carry an unspoken belief in an intrinsic good in all. Some believe that we each carry a divine spark that links us to a greater good/the divine creator. Yet, with the increasing breakdown of society, mainstream beliefs have been shaken.

Nonetheless a growing minority treasure the belief that things are getting better. It depends on your perspective. Do you try to sense how we are awakening internally, or do you allow all manner of external news to sway you from your centre? At the end of an era, we find ourselves straddling two or more belief systems. Do we swing at times between optimism and despair. The stage is set for a massive shift in collective consciousness. We are becoming more responsible for creating Heaven on Earth. We are in the first tentative stages of becoming co-creators.

Trees presented the root material within a long thread of wisdom traditions. Could it be that we have to revisit the trees and reinvent the wheel for our times? If we are to help the Earth in her hour of need, we can do worse than commune with our trees again. We must do so from a standpoint of fuller consciousness than our predecessors. How do we view the trees from a modern spiritual viewpoint?

Concluding Remarks

In the booklet "Tree Murmurs" I composed a poem for each tree. It represented the qualities perceived by the ancient peoples. In many ways I saw these poems as soul poems, tapping into the soul of each tree. I sensed a universal truth lay in the knowledge contained in the poem. I still find that for many who read their birth tree, the poem speaks to them. Seventeen years on from when I wrote *Tree Murmurs*, I see the whole cycle from a more holistic viewpoint, in which each tree plays a vital role. Nowadays, anyone can tap into this inner world of magic the trees contain. I offer workshops to enable people to do so. When we make a more conscious connection with trees, a kind of memory emerges by which we can decode the tree. We can choose to acknowledge that nature spirits inhabit the trees. Merlin energy helps our relationship with nature, rather than our actions with men. Merlin lived among the world of the trees, for the trees communicated at a deep, psychic level with him. They satisfied his soul's elemental yearning. From this communion he was able to enter into a telepathic state. There was a mutual sharing of energies. Our consciousness is now opening up to many dimensions that had been closed to us in the last millennia or more. We are now able to emulate this approach. We can rekindle an energetic field of communication with trees, of relevance in the world. For nature needs our loving attention. It helps to release it from trauma and evolve in its own way.

Man's relations with one another holds parallels to mankind's relationship with nature. If we can work with the "Merlin" energy through our own humble efforts, we will realize its relevance. The return of Merlin is about creating a transformed relationship with nature. We could actively work with nature, particularly trees, and accept the peace she offers.

I encourage you to experience and enjoy sharing your new found tree wisdom. Actively coming together for such a purpose is a definite upgrade of the old Druidic system. That society imposed a hierarchy on knowledge that only a select few in society could access. Now we choose from inner freedom to follow any path that leads us to the divine. Modern morality is self-imposed. It springs from the heart which is open and a mind that holds equilibrium. The message is simple and yet still hard to achieve from moment to moment. Love connects us with the ALL. The tree meditations offer glimpses of eternal codes of light that still serve us today. The notion of a co-operative cycle of tree souls can assist our growth.

Appendix

Fabian Maman (*www.tama-do.com*) a leading researcher and teacher of sound healing.

Marko Pogačnik (*www.markopogacnik.com/*) a leading geomancer, writer and UNESCO Artist for Peace.

Jackie Queally (*www.earthwise.me*) spiritual writer, tour guide, sound therapist and Ogham essence practitioner. Contact her at *jackiequeally@gmail.com* for talks and workshops on the Celtic Trees

https://www.facebook.com/earthwiseconnect/

www.ingramcontent.com/pod-product-compliance
Lightning Source LLC
Chambersburg PA
CBHW070452090426
42735CB00012B/2526